D1036005

John Christgau

Birch Coulie
The Epic Battle of the Dakota War

University of Nebraska Press   *Lincoln & London*

Library of Congress Cataloging-in-Publication Data
Christgau, John.
Birch Coulie: the epic battle of the Dakota war / John Christgau.
p. cm.
Includes bibliographical references.
ISBN 978-0-8032-3636-3 (pbk.: alk. paper)
1. Birch Coulee, Battle of, Minn., 1862. 2. Dakota Indians—Wars, 1862–1865. 3. Minnesota—History—1858– I. Title.
E83.86.C47 2012
973.7′476—dc23
2011032553

Set in ITC New Baskerville by Bob Reitz.

Contents

Preface

The Battle of Birch Coulie and the Dakota War of 1862 were extraordinary events in American history. In the days following the battle and the war, one of President Lincoln's private secretaries wrote that "there has hardly been an outbreak so treacherous, so sudden, so bitter, and so bloody, as that which filled the State of Minnesota with sorrow and lamentation."

It was war waged so fiercely and dramatically that the issues and controversies underlying it would persist long after the conflict ended. The decades-long court battle to see the eventual restoration of annuity payments to the Dakotas resurrected disagreements from the war between those who argued that the annuity system only led to a government paternalism that frustrated Indian independence and those who argued that without economic help Indian nations would disappear.

As the twentieth century drew to a close, what the white man called "education," however well-intentioned, continued to threaten Native American culture. Whether or not to receive education at the hands of the white man was framed as a choice between ending Indian poverty by joining the American mainstream in which there was no room for Indian customs and beliefs and that "ground away at what made Indian people different," or preserving Indian heritage at the risk of separatism. By the 1980s that choice would split Native American communities into "ethnic Indians" versus "tribal Indians." That same division had separated the "cut-hairs" from the "blanket Indians" in the Dakota War.

Succeeding generations, not just of Minnesotans but all Americans, were torn between admiration for their hardy white ancestors who had carved farms and towns out of the frontier and regret for how Indian culture and history had been nearly destroyed in order to build those white settlements. After the Dakota War that equivocation hung in the air for decades like a moral smog. Yet in 2009, with a black president and a New America supposedly enlightened about race, there were those who clung to the stereotypes of the Dakota War and insisted that the Indians who had nearly wiped out 153 soldiers at Birch Coulie were nothing but "Fighting Sioux," a bloodthirsty and warlike race.

Author's Note

A precise timetable for Birch Coulie and the Dakota War is difficult to determine. The various eyewitness accounts of events vary by hours, in some cases days. Where the confusion is unresolvable, I have incorporated the timetable that best serves my intention to present a dramatic narrative.

The Battle of Birch Coulie unfolded with the tension and histrionics of a hair-raising melodrama. To capture that sense of drama, I frequently rendered the action through dialogue. That dialogue appears here exactly as it appears in battle accounts and reminiscences. Or it is language just as it appears in the rendering of specific scenes in those same accounts and reminiscences.

Birch Coulie

1.

Private Robert K. Boyd

THE SOLDIERS COULD HAVE BEEN MISTAKEN FOR A picnic party, laughing as they marched merrily in a column across the Minnesota prairie, drinking from the creeks and streams they crossed, and gathering ripe fruit from trees on homesteads that had been abandoned by fleeing settlers. Then they came across the bodies of the first settlers who had been shot with arrows. The corpses had lain in the hot prairie sun for two weeks and were bloated and maggoty. As the men dug graves for the victims, they were no longer picnickers on a prairie romp but a burial detail charged with the most gruesome work any of them had ever done.

It was the morning of August 31, 1862. They were a contingent of 153 men drawn mainly from the Sixth Minnesota Volunteer Regiment. The detail included a complement of fifty "home guard" cavalry and two dozen civilians in search of missing friends. The detail also included nearly two dozen wagons with teamsters.

The burial detail moved north from Fort Ridgely, which

had been built on a bluff above the Minnesota River in 1853 in western Minnesota and which was intended to be a frontier redoubt against the very events that were now occurring. The soldiers had been directed to find and bury the bodies of numerous prairie settlers who had been killed in the previous two weeks by warring Dakota Indians.

Each man of the expedition carried two days' rations, paper cartridges with gunpowder, percussion caps, and forty rounds of ammunition in his pockets. An additional three thousand rounds of ammunition had been packed into wooden boxes and loaded onto wagons. For drill at Fort Snelling, the men had been issued Belgian muskets that were described as "inaccurate and worthless." At St. Peter, Minnesota, the men had been issued Springfield rifle muskets, which most of them now carried.

Who had been assigned to lead the burial party was a matter of dispute. Some of the men felt it was thirty-four-year-old Captain Hiram P. Grant, a Sixth Regiment volunteer officer. A native of Vermont, Grant had moved to St. Paul in 1855 and had no experience on the frontier or in fighting Indians.

Other soldiers felt that the leader of the expedition was Major Joseph R. Brown, a portly frontier trader who had served in the House of Representatives. Brown had been on a trip to Chicago when he learned of the Dakota outbreak. His nineteen-room home on reservation lands had been destroyed, and his family had been captured, so he had not hesitated to accept a commission in the newly formed militia.

Brown had also been the inventor of a self-propelled steam wagon. But at the first test of the huge machine—a trial run from Henderson, Minnesota, to Fort Ridgely—it had belched smoke and steam and then sunk in the mud. Despite the failure, Brown remained resourceful and exuded self-confidence and authority. Part of that authority included being "well posted in the signs and character of Indians," and his men said that he could "smell Indians from afar." Before the burial party had set out, Captain Grant had been told that if he needed advice, he was to consult "Major" Brown.

Although Brown was a civilian whose appointment as U.S. Indian agent for the Dakotas had just ended, he outranked Captain Grant, and therefore some of the men felt he was the expedition's leader. He had an Indian wife and traveled freely between the Indian and white communities. Brown had a prominent nose and thick, coarse hair that curled over his ears like surf, and his hard face reflected that he feared nothing, least of all Indians among whom he had spent much of his life. Since his own wife and children had been taken captive by the Dakotas, he was eager to see that the expedition did its burial duties swiftly and then turned its attention to discovering the whereabouts of the Indians and their captives.

No soldier worked harder at the grim business of burying bodies than an eighteen-year-old ruddy Scotsman, Private Robert K. Boyd. As a boy Boyd had come east from Illinois with his family and settled in St. Charles, Minnesota, where he attended a one-room schoolhouse. He and his older class-mates listened with fascination as recruiters and prominent local citizens from St. Charles urged young men to answer President Lincoln's call for Civil War volunteers. To demon-strate to his schoolmates his readiness to go to battle, Boyd invited them to stick pins or a knifepoint in his arms while he pretended to feel no pain. It was, he knew, a woeful test of his fitness for the pain of battle, but the act reflected how desperate he was to join the Union Army.

"If they don't get enough soldiers," he told his parents, "I should go."

They greeted his announcement with horse laughs.

Late in the summer of 1861, a wounded veteran of the First Battle of Bull Run had come to St. Charles and told thrilling stories of his combat adventures. Boyd spent the subsequent winter and spring dreaming of battle and telling himself, "If I don't see my share of it, I'll hate myself all my life."

One night in June 1862, at seventeen, he ran away from home. With one set of clothes and no money or food, he ate chokecherries and gooseberries to survive. He swam the roaring Whitewater River, climbed a sheer three-hundred-foot cliff, and using only the North Star as a guide, he made his way to Fort Snelling in St. Paul, where he enlisted in the Sixth Minnesota Volunteer Regiment, then being formed.

For six weeks Boyd had trained at Fort Snelling. Then on the morning of August 18 news had reached the fort of the Indian depredations on the frontier. Boyd's regiment had relieved the garrison at Fort Ridgely.

On the morning of the formation of the burial detail, Boyd had slipped away to the river valley to pick wild grapes. He heard the bugle call to fall in and was still bearing clumps of grapes in his hand when he was the last to join the ranks of his company. For his tardy appearance in the formation, his company commander had thought to punish him by assigning him along with several other troopers to the burial detail.

Boyd hadn't even had time to sight and fire the new Springfield rifle musket he had been issued, so he wasn't sure of what use he would be as a rifleman. But all his young life he had dreamed of adventure, and he took pride in the belief that nothing could shock him or unnerve him. In any case, the burial expedition didn't promise the pitched battle of First Bull Run, with cannon smoke and fixed bayonets and the blood-curdling yells of Rebel troops. Still, the chance to go into dangerous Indian country was just the adventure Robert K. Boyd was seeking.

The expedition buried dozens of settlers that first day out. Many of the corpses were mutilated and ghastly, and some of the men assigned to the digging became too distraught to continue the work. But Boyd did not back away from laying even the most ravaged corpses into freshly dug graves.

At one point during the work, Captain Grant passed on horseback and stopped to watch Boyd's furious grave-digging pace. After a moment he beckoned Boyd to approach him. Boyd did as directed, saluted, and then stood at attention.

"What's your name?" Grant asked.

"Private Robert K. Boyd, sir."

"What company?"

"Company F, sir."

"I've watched you work, Private."

Boyd remained silent at attention.

"You've done your share. I wish I had more men like you in my command."

Boyd had never in his life received a compliment, not even as brief as the one Grant had just delivered. He turned red now but managed to stammer, "Sir, I always try to do the best I can."

Grant rode off and Boyd returned to the grim work. But Captain Grant's compliment had convinced him that he was no longer just a pretender to leathery toughness. His courage was the real thing. He had never much cared for the opinion of others, but Grant's praise had changed him "from a boy into a man." He vowed he would give his superiors absolute loyalty, "and if a battle comes, I will fight regardless of danger . . . to the limit of my strength and endurance."

While the grave diggers worked, a party of scouts detached from the burial party rode farther north in search of the warring Indians. They found nothing but deserted Indian villages.

When the scouts caught up with the burial party in the late afternoon, they reported to Grant, "The Indians have left."

Grant wanted to know how long ago.

"We think four days ago," they told him.

"Couldn't you have followed their tracks?"

"Yes, but it would have been slow. They would have scattered and followed the ridges where the grass is short and the ground is hard. It makes for false tracks."

"So where do you think they have gone?" Grant asked.

"We don't know."

"Don't you think they have all gone west to buffalo country?"

"They might have done that," the scouts conceded.

Then Major Brown offered his opinion. "The Indians have become frightened by the presence of white troops in their country," he said with his usual authority. "They have gone west to the James River with their plunder and prisoners."

With a party of several men, Major Brown went to the top of the river bluffs to look for a safe place to camp that night. While they scouted the terrain, one of the young soldiers back with the main expedition spotted what he thought were Indians in the distance across the river moving south. The soldier quickly tried to call the attention of his fellow infantrymen to what he saw, but the Indians were only visible for a minute or two, and the soldier's observations were dismissed as the frightened hallucinations of a green recruit.

Brown argued for camping that night on a Minnesota River bluff at the head of Beaver Creek. He instructed his cavalry detachment to water their horses in the creek, then ascend to the bluff for camping. But Captain Grant had already halted his column on the valley floor beneath the high bluffs. It was, he felt, the appropriate place to camp. It meant that Brown and the cavalry detachment had to move back down to the valley floor, where they grumbled over Grant's selection of a vulnerable spot for camping. One of the cavalry men pointed to the high bluffs. The Indians would "be able to shoot the life out of every one of us from up there," he said.

The soldiers then laid out their bedrolls with a wary eye

to those surrounding bluffs. But Captain Grant reassured them that they were just as safe as if they were in their own homes.

Grant instructed one of his lieutenants to post night pickets. But a check of those pickets revealed that one of them didn't even know the password for the night. It did not "accord well," Grant felt.

"Well, it is all right now," the lieutenant assured Grant.

A bugler sounded tattoo, the signal for all quiet. But one of the soldiers spit on another's rifle, and the subsequent scuffle kept the men awake. Finally, the men fell asleep under a starry sky, battling horrible nightmares of mutilated and burned corpses. Some of them were so fearful of attack that they slept with muskets cocked, ready to fire.

After a restless night's sleep with one eye on the threatening bluffs overlooking their encampment, the expedition's bugler sounded reveille at dawn to awaken the men for the second day of the grisly burial work. Grateful to have made it through the night without incident in their vulnerable campsite, the men were talkative and cheerful as they moved in a long file up out of the river valley.

The first suspicion that Indians were nearby came from a half-blood corporal with the expedition named Joseph Coursolle, a thirty-two-year-old blacksmith who was the son of a French-Canadian trader and a Dakota mother. Coursolle, his wife Marie, and his three children, including nine-day-old Little Joe, had been living with other mixed-bloods on the reservation known as the Lower Agency when it had been attacked two weeks earlier. Coursolle and his family had tried to escape at night in a dugout down the Minnesota River. But Indians had chased them, and while the two daughters, Elizabeth six and Minnie four, hid in the river bank bushes, Coursolle had fled downriver with his wife and baby, who during the ordeal had turned pale and sickly.

The refugees found shelter at Fort Ridgely. Once in the safety of the fort, Little Joe had grown weaker and died. For Coursolle the idea that he could lose all three of his children in just a few weeks had been unthinkable. He had been determined to return some twenty miles north to the Lower Agency and learn the fate of his two little girls. The formation of the burial party of soldiers had been just the opportunity he was looking for, and he was one of the first to volunteer.

"Don't worry," he told Marie as the expedition headed out, "I will bring back Elizabeth and Minnie."

As the expedition moved up out of the river valley, Coursolle spotted fresh piles of kinnikinick, or bearberry branches, that had been stripped of their bark. The leaves of the bush, Coursolle knew, were prized by Indians for their healing properties. They could be boiled into a powerful, astringent tea. They were also often mixed with other leaves and smoked. But the stripped bark of the branches meant something else to Coursolle. That bark made excellent wadding for muskets, better even than paper, and Coursolle often used it himself.

His fears of nearby gun-bearing Indians were one thing. It was what every man in the burial party felt, and it proved nothing concerning the whereabouts of the Dakotas. But the piles of kinnikinick branches, with fresh footprints around them, were a different matter. They convinced Coursolle that the Indians were very close.

As soon as the column reached the river bluffs, more suspicions were aroused when one of Grant's soldiers at the tail end of the column thought he heard the boom of firearms from down in the timber along the river. Then he spotted three suspicious puffs of smoke rising from the bluffs across the river.

Major Brown rode back from the head of the column to listen to the soldier's suspicions. Was it possible, the soldier wondered, that the smoke was a signal by Indians that the expedition had been discovered moving up out of the river flats?

"What you take to be smoke," Brown told the soldier, "is road dust caused by little whirlwinds."

The expedition moved out onto the prairie and continued the work of burying dead settlers. Of all the grisly burials they did that day, the worst was of Mrs. J. R. Henderson, a young woman with two children. She and her children had been among a party of twenty-seven settlers headed south to the safety of Fort Ridgely. By removing the back seats from a spring wagon, a soft feather bed with pillows was made for the gravely ill Mrs. Henderson and her children. But within five minutes of starting for Fort Ridgely, the party had been stopped by a line of Dakota soldiers stretched across the cart trail. Mrs. Henderson removed one of the white pillow cases and waved it as a flag of truce. Despite the gesture the Dakotas pulled Mrs. Henderson and her two children from the wagon, shot the three of them, then threw them on the feather bed, which had been set afire.

The sight of the burned corpses brought a new round of revulsion to the burial party. Two harmless, sweet children mutilated and then burned! For the members of the burial party, it was an indication of how ruthless the Indians had become.

The burial party dug small neat graves for the Henderson children. As Corporal Joseph Coursolle dug in the hot sun, he was stricken with the fear that the perpetrators were still lurking close by. He had seen their tracks around the kinnikinick bushes. They could be waiting to pounce on the gravediggers, Coursolle thought. Meanwhile, his baby son Little Joe was already dead. Now, as he helped bury the Henderson children, he was unable to shake the nightmare vision of the eyes of his two little girls, perhaps lying dead somewhere on the prairie. He was even stricken with visions of how his own body would look if the expedition were surrounded and all were killed by Indians.

It was when they were traveling again as a column across the prairie that Captain Grant spotted strange movements in the deep grass ahead. It was, he thought, an Indian dropping down into the grass.

Grant detailed twenty men to race ahead and kill the Indian. But as soon as they reached the spot in the grass where Grant had seen the suspicious activity, the detail discovered an even worse victim than any they had buried. And this one was alive.

Her name was Justina Kreiger, twenty-eight, and just two weeks earlier she and the members of the German community around Sacred Heart, Minnesota, had gathered to flee as a group to nearby Fort Ridgely. The Indians had intercepted their passage and directed them to go back to their homes. Once there, she had watched with horror as her family's homestead was burned and her husband and three children were killed. Before his death her husband directed her to flee, but she had gone only twenty yards before the Indians fired buckshot into her back. Then they cut off her clothes, sliced a four-inch gash in her stomach, and left her for dead on the prairie.

She had wandered the prairie in a daze for over a week, eating berries and drinking from small streams. To the burial party she seemed on the edge of death and pointed repeatedly to her shoulder as the site of a serious wound, but it was only a slight flesh wound made by a tomahawk. Captain Grant wrapped her in a blanket and carried her back to a grass bed improvised in one of the wagons of the expedition.

It was now late afternoon, and Grant realized he could not travel the twenty-two miles back to Fort Ridgely before nightfall. Instead, Grant led the expedition in a file that moved east across the prairie as he searched for a campsite that would offer water and wood.

It was on the open prairie alongside Birch Coulie that he chose a spot for his expedition to camp the second night. "Coulie" was a French term for a dry or watery streambed with steep slopes. Birch Coulie was sixty feet deep and had been carved ten thousand years earlier as a conduit for the melt water of the last ice age. It originated on the flat prairie and ran for seven miles before its waters emptied into the Minnesota River, then the Mississippi, and finally the Gulf of Mexico.

The coulie slopes were covered with birch, small oak trees, and dry brush. The Dakotas called it Tanpa Yukan, or the "Place of the White Birch." Before he had set out from Fort Ridgely, Grant had received instruction from his superiors to "avoid any pass or defile" where the party might be waylaid or ambushed. The site beside Birch Coulie was high ground, and it seemed an unlikely place for an ambush. In addition, there was wood and water just to the east. Over the course of two days, Grant's men had buried fifty-four settlers. After such grisly work the flat, soft ground on the prairie beside the coulie would give the tired troops an opportunity for a comfortable night's sleep. Finally, the open prairie to the north and west provided a clear field of vision against the possibility of a surprise attack.

But exactly those qualities that recommended the site to Grant were what made it vulnerable. The coulie ravine was just such a defile as he had been warned against. It provided a natural breastworks and shield in which attackers could remain close but hidden. A thick woods to the south also provided cover for would-be attackers. And the deep prairie grass to the north and west of the site offered a screen through which Indians could crawl and be almost upon the expedition and its wagons before revealing themselves. Finally, a gentle knoll just one hundred yards away in that west grass was a vantage point for sniper fire and the gathering of forces.

Several of Grant's men felt that a campsite just a few yards from the natural defile of a coulie was too dangerous. Grant's response was to move the site back two hundred yards. Then he directed his teamsters to form a protective horseshoe of wagons on the open prairie, with the mouth of the horseshoe facing the coulie to the east. He picketed the cavalry horses and wagon teams to a long rope run between the wagons. There were a total of ninety-six animals picketed around the edge of the horseshoe.

Inside the horseshoe Grant's men threw up Sibley tents, which were shaped like teepees and which could sleep fifteen to twenty men. Those for whom there wasn't enough room in the tents threw out their bedrolls next to the wagons and under the stars.

At sunset Major Brown and the detachment of cavalry that had ridden north to scout again for Indians joined Grant's encampment beside Birch Coulie. One of Major Brown's cavalry officers, Captain Joe Anderson, had fought in the Mexican War. The balding Anderson knew how critical site selection was for bivouacking troops, and he felt that Birch Coulie was a dangerous campsite. However, he was told to dismount and eat, after which he would feel better. Still, Anderson carried his anxieties to bed with him and instructed one of his cooks who would be up before dawn to wake him immediately if the cook heard anything suspicious.

A full moon cast a silver crust on the wagons. The stillness and the thick smell of the dead prairie grass made the landscape seem inert, lifeless. As Joe Coursolle laid out his bedroll in a shallow pit he had dug beneath one of the wagons, he thought he should report his kinnikinick observations to his company sergeant. "You better give the information to Captain Grant," he told the sergeant.

But instead of reporting Coursolle's suspicions to Grant,

the sergeant alerted Major Brown, who ignored Coursolle's warning. Meanwhile, Captain Grant established ten three-man picket posts around the Birch Coulie encampment. Each post was twenty yards outside the horseshoe of wagons, and the men were ordered to stay awake and be on guard.

The same bugler who sounded reveille now delivered a melancholy tattoo. The men inside the encampment loaded their muskets and laid them beside them before they attempted to fall asleep.

Finally, Major Brown walked among the anxious men, who he knew were facing another night of horrible nightmares of corpses and burning buildings. Their anxiety was palpable, and Brown did his best to reassure them. "Go to sleep," he told the troops. "Don't worry about Indians. There are none within a hundred miles." Then he added the most comforting reassurance he could think of. "There is no more danger here than in your mother's house." With that assurance most of the men fell asleep immediately, little aware, if at all, of how events had roused an Indian anger that would soon be focused entirely on the expedition in the hope of wiping it out.

2.

Red Iron

No one in the mid-nineteenth century was
sure where these strange Indian people had come from. At
the time some argued that their origins were as mysterious
as the dawn of life itself. Others insisted that the Indians
had come in an ancient migration from Asia before the land
bridge to North America had been swamped by the rising
waters of the Bering Sea.

In North American the Indians wandered and scattered.
The Sioux, of whom the Dakotas were part, were thought to
have settled first in the Carolinas. Then the encroachment of
the white man pushed them east to the Ohio Valley, finally
to the wilderness of the upper Midwest. From there some of
them had fled still farther west. Explorers who encountered
the Sioux who remained in the upper Midwest described
them as wretched and diseased. Their tribes were ravaged
by smallpox, brought to them and other tribes by the white
man. Indeed, by the 1830s what had been millions of Indians in North America had been reduced to just two million

souls who tried to imitate the white man while swallowing his alcohol poison. Indian orators spoke with an uncharacteristic fatalism. "We know," they said, "that the white men are like a great cloud that rises in the East and will cover the whole country." Meanwhile, white writers wrote poignantly, "so the aborigines pass away, and the few survivors in our land may chant in sorrow."

Doomed or not, the Indians were the objects of curiosity. Explorers and scholars and artists came into the wilderness by steamboat and canoe to study their "manners and customs and conditions." These observers described Indians, the Sioux among them, as profoundly religious, although some white men dismissed belief in a Great Spirit as mere superstition. All objects, many Indians believed, were sacred and had a spiritual existence. Some even prayed to stones. Many Indians believed that at death, if the mortal had been good, his or her soul left the body and traveled to a region of eternal happiness. If the individual had been bad, the soul drowned. It was a faith whose promises also were at the core of Christianity. Yet there were those in the nineteenth century who felt the Indian needed to be converted from his savage existence to the white man's faith. But Indian medicine men were more influential than priests, and efforts to teach the Indians about Christianity brought few converts.

The first white pioneers in the new land described the Indian as a "merry creature." In the eyes of these pioneers, he was agile and playful and walked in moccasins with the nonchalance of a child and the dignity of a man. He laughed at the white man, who he said walked like a dandy in clodhoppers and entered a teepee like a frog. The white man, he said, was a sad creature because he had lost his agility in his effort to acquire power. Meanwhile, nineteenth-century observers claimed that Indians loved games and could romp half-naked with "serpentine ease and deerlike swiftness" from sunup to sundown across an endless sward, using a long stick with a webbed pocket to hurl a tiny ball through a makeshift goal.

Indians were tribal, with many living in villages close to water. "We cannot dig wells like the white man," they explained. "We must have our home by the flowing rivers." Many believed that polygamy was authorized by the Great Spirit, and they did not understand the white man's habit of taking only one wife. Indians often fought with courage and bravery in short-lived feuds, the purpose of which was as much to touch the enemy as to kill him. No people were more attached to the land of their birth. They believed that the land and the rocks were made of Indian flesh, and if the white man seized it in his never-ending desire for earthly possessions, it left a hole in Indian flesh, and "the blood would never stop running."

It was the white man's everlasting desire to possess the earth and its creatures that brought the first explorers and a few settlers to the upper Mississippi. The area was described as "paradise," and despite being fired upon by Indians, settlers came by wagon and steamboat to work the soil, persuaded in part by Thomas Jefferson's assurances that the cultivators of the earth were its most valuable citizens. Their "manifest destiny" was to occupy North America.

The first settlers who came to the Minnesota Territory were hardy Swedes who did their best to clear the rocks and stumps for farming in a triangle of land between the St. Croix and Mississippi Rivers. They found impenetrable woods and howling, icy winters. There were savage Indians "skulking" in those deep woods. By 1850 there were less than four thousand pioneers scattered in lonely outposts in the territory.

In an effort to lure more settlers and to fatten the treasury of the government and the wallets of land profiteers, promoters hailed the Minnesota Territory as a land covered with the richest soil. The windswept prairie was described as limitless and fertile. "No one ever died in Minnesota," the profiteers wrote, "except two men, one of whom was hanged for killing the other." The prediction was that the beauty and richness of the land would soon bring a "great wave of migration."

Still, few came. Among those who did were traders and profiteers and missionaries. For the traders there was money to be made in purchasing blankets in St. Louis for $3.25, then trading them to the Indians for muskrat skins worth three times that amount. There was also money to be made by harvesting fat fish from deep blue lakes.

The missionaries came to wean the Indians from their spiritual beliefs and save Indian souls. Only a few white writers saw the irony that Christianity, which had waded through a "sea of blood," was now trying to teach goodness and love. But the missionaries remained determined to see that the "juggleries and sorceries" of the Indian medicine men were abandoned. Indians should adopt the habits of white men and live in fixed homes like farmers. As an incentive the Indians were given farm implements, two pigs, and seeds for planting. But little of the evangelical spirit took hold among the tribes of the Sioux, who did not try to convert others to their way of life. So why should *they* be converted?

Along with the missionaries came the profiteers and swindlers with a host of sins. Their wish to keep the "savages" ignorant so that they could be cheated seemed at cross-purposes to the work of the missionaries. On the one hand, the white man's presumption of power and imperialism was irritating. On the other, it was also intimidating. "Your people have become very great," an Indian chief observed about white men. "Our people have become very small."

For the new settlers in the triangle of land, the prospect of clearing the land of boulders and stumps seemed daunting. Meanwhile, there was fertile, rich prairie land that invited settlement and farming in southern and southwestern Minnesota. The trouble was that it was Dakota land. However, the government went again to its bag of treaty tricks to persuade the Dakotas to sell their land.

The deal was struck on a muggy July day in 1851 at a shallow narrows called Traverse des Sioux along the Minnesota River, where the Dakotas crossed to hunt and fish. Under a shade canopy of boughs, the white man's imperial power was evident, and the Dakota chiefs and headmen were led by the government's "knavery and deception" and outright fraud into signing what would eventually be called the Treaty of Traverse des Sioux, which sold off their ancestral lands.

The ceremony began festively, with two thousand people gathered to watch, including government officials, traders in coonskin caps, chiefs cradling peace pipes in one arm, journalists, poets, artists sketching furiously, and hundreds of tribesmen. There was a city of teepees and military tents. Journalists described the event as a "riot of feasting" on pork and beef, with dances, beating drums, footraces, and games of lacrosse. There were weeks of solemn speeches and serious deliberations. The Dakota children were warned to stay away from negotiations being held under the bough canopy. There were predictions that the peace and friendship "so happily existing" between the United States and Indians would last forever. Finally, one by one, the chiefs signed the treaty laid out on a barrel head.

Several days later, another treaty ceremony was held at Mendota, Minnesota. This time, there was even more of a sense of government imperialism. The second treaty seemed almost inevitable, and the chiefs eventually signed away still more southern Minnesota land to the government.

The terms of the Traverse des Sioux and Mendota treaties stipulated that the Dakotas would cede to the U.S. government twenty-four million acres of "vast and undulating plains" for $1.6 million, which amounted to twelve and a half cents an acre. The huge land purchase by the government resurrected an old frontier saying: "When you are gettin', get aplenty." In addition to the treaties, at Traverse des Sioux there were also "traders papers" that the chiefs signed but didn't understand. The papers required the tribes to use much of the government money to pay off debts to the traders for food and other provisions.

It wasn't long before the chiefs, stung by the criticism of their tribesmen, realized they had been cheated. But only a few white voices were raised in objection to the treaties. An Episcopal bishop described the Traverse des Sioux Treaty as a "mask for naked conquest" by the white man. But defenders of the two treaties again called it manifest destiny, part of America's inevitable western movement. To whites of the mid-nineteenth century, the Caucasian race was the superior race of the world. Wearing a laurel wreath and a sash sprinkled with white stars, Columbia, the female personification of America, would lead civilization west, stringing telegraph wires as she went. "Give way, young warriors," a frontier poet wrote about the new lands, "the white man claims them now." Railroads and cities with skyscrapers would soon replace the Indians. Their horses and dogs would fade and then vanish.

The U.S. Senate refused to ratify the treaties until the Dakotas agreed to be "relocated" to reservations. Meanwhile, twenty thousand immigrants squatted illegally on the new unsurveyed lands. But no one threw them off. They were described as a "great army of peaceful progress" who made the country's "history and glory."

With final approval of the treaties, seven thousand Dakotas ended up relocated to the Upper Sioux Agency and the Lower Sioux Agency, which were thirty miles apart on a narrow strip of land alongside the Minnesota River. It was confinement that made sense to the white man because the Indian was uncivilized. Dakotas were said to "have the least reason in their composition." They were a "savage and ferocious people" who buried their dead on prairie scaffolds. They subscribed to a weird religion and did mad dances. They were cruel by nature and harbored an instinctive hatred of whites that was meant to prevent their subjugation to the great Caucasian mind.

More chiefs joined in protest over the treaties. "It was the land of my fathers," one of them lamented. "I had reason to love it. The Americans came and demanded my lands. They were supposed to give us money and goods . . . but nothing reached my hand more than a few dollars." Other chiefs tried to undo the treaties. Chief Red Iron was leader of one of the largest Dakota bands. With long braids, a bonnet of two cocked feather, and a "body beaming with intelligence and resolution," he complained to territorial governor Alexander Ramsey that at Traverse de Sioux traders had "thrown blankets over our faces and darkened our eyes, and got us to sign papers we did not understand."

The governor's response was sharp. "You have acted badly," the governor said, "and I do break you."

It was more of the white man's irritating imperialism, and Red Iron shot back, "You break *me?* My *people* made me a chief!"

For the Dakotas, Traverse des Sioux and Mendota became just more treaties with the white man, "as worthless as a rope of sand." In anticipation of the huge land acquisition, five thousand settlers had been poised to invade Indian lands, treaties or no. With the treaties now in place, there was a sense of legitimacy to the invasion. Already surveyors had laid out six-mile-square townships, which were in turn broken into 650-acre sections for sale at auction. But the price seemed overwhelming to the "cultivators of the earth," and very little land sold. Halving the ownership parcels to 320 acres didn't work either. Finally, the government chopped the sections into 80-acre parcels that could be purchased at $1.25 an acre. In the meantime, enterprising white men opened roads, cut timber, built sawmills and houses, dammed rivers and creeks, and platted towns with lots ready to accommodate 1.5 million settlers.

Land fever erupted. From 1851 to 1860 a million German immigrants, double the number of the previous decade, came to the United States seeking their fortunes. In the new Minnesota Territory 150,000 hopeful immigrants poured onto the land. St. Paul hotels became so crowded that the new arrivals slept in the streets. In two years the number of steamboats carrying settlers up the Minnesota River to stake land claims or to populate the frontier villages nearly tripled. But the settlers found only paper lots in town sites that existed nowhere except on maps. With foreclosures on worthless property and subsequent bank failures, the land boom crashed down as fast as it had been thrown together.

Still new arrivals came. With statehood for Minnesota in 1858, more immigrants arrived. It left two very different peoples living in "mutual ignorance of each other" along a frontier that ran from the Lake of the Woods in Minnesota to the Gulf of Mexico. Life along that frontier was filled with misfortune and calamity and "lawless iniquity." The Indians were "kicked about like dogs and beaten into a sort of civilization." On their new reservations the Dakotas were expected to break the land and build fences like white farmers. Money promised for education and schools would be distributed at the direction of the president. But the Dakotas confined to lands with little timber and no game wanted food, not spelling books. No matter, they were told that their fate was to learn to live with the white man.

Unscrupulous traders and land profiteers along that frontier spread dissipation and distrust among the Indians. It made the white man's lectures about goodness and love seem even more hypocritical. Those missionaries still in search of Indian souls to convert were told they had a better chance of finding converts among the innocent, trusting savages deeper in the wilderness.

A few more critical voices were raised among the white man. They insisted that the whole annuity system had a "paralyzing and stupefying" effect on Indians. The critics charged that the profiteers and government officials had no idea how to deal with an unsophisticated people who were being destroyed. These people deserved sympathy and a helping hand. "We have broken up their tribal relations," one critic accused, "and they must have something in their place." But what had replaced their "vast undulating prairie" was a narrow strip of land as confining as a prison. In that prison the Dakotas were expected to learn to farm and work the land. But west of the reservation, from British Columbia to Texas, there were vast herds of buffalo to be hunted, and many of the Dakotas only returned to the two agencies to receive their annual annuities.

An eventual promise of free land drew still more settlers to Minnesota, and Dakota frustration and anger grew. In June 1861 the writer Henry David Thoreau, who had come up the Minnesota River by steamboat to observe the annual annuity payments, noted that the Dakotas were deeply unhappy. Then that fall an invasion of cut worms meant the harvest for the Indians who tried to take up farming was slim. Winter brought one of the coldest spells in Minnesota history. For weeks temperatures sank to thirty and forty below zero, with furious blizzards and deep snow. In the spring of 1862 more heavy snows made the prairie too deep with snowdrifts for hunting. The "breeches Indians" and "cut-heads" (also known as "cut-hairs"), who had adopted the white man's clothing and habits of grooming, were struggling to grow crops. The Dakotas began to look gaunt and desperate, and many of the bands resorted to eating roots.

At this time, the Union defeat in July at First Bull Run made Congress anxious about more funding for the war.

Officials in Washington dithered over whether to send annuity payments to Minnesota in paper or gold. Back on the two reservations in Minnesota, all the dogs had been eaten, and the Dakotas turned to eating raw corn and hunting for teepson, or wild turnips. "We are hungry," the Dakotas complained to traders who managed warehouses of food, "and we want beef."

The annual annuities came in two forms: goods and cash. The annuity goods, including food, had already arrived and awaited distribution. But the cash annuities were late. Eager to avoid the paper work of two separate distributions to the Indians, Agent Thomas J. Galbraith insisted on waiting for the arrival of the cash before he gave out the food. The hungry Indians would have to wait.

Five thousand Dakotas were now camped at the Upper Agency. It was time to take matters into their own hands, and they broke into the warehouses and carried out flour. Finally Galbraith provided them with crackers, and the Dakotas "crawled over each other" and rushed for the food like "wildcats."

On July 26 the Dakotas were told to prepare for their annuity payments. However, a headcount would have to be made first. It led to a "sea of Indians . . . squaws, papooses, dogs, horses, carts, red, white and blue blankets . . . a mass of confusion." Still, in anticipation of the cash and food, the Dakotas were described as gleeful. But the cash still failed to arrive, and the Dakota glee disappeared. Tensions rose still further, and on August 2 a small squad of soldiers arrived at the Upper Agency with a mountain howitzer to keep order.

Despite the presence of the soldiers, 1,500 Dakotas surrounded one of the warehouses and fired their guns. Then they again began to break into the warehouse. They were ordered to "fall back" or the cannon would blow them all to hell.

The Dakotas fell back immediately, but they pleaded, "We

are the braves. We have sold our lands to our great father and we think he intends to give us what he has promised. But we can't get it if we are starving. We want something to eat."

Agent Galbraith's response to the impasse that he had created was to treat the Dakotas as if they had been *unwilling* to eat, and he issued an order requiring "the Sioux Indians to at once accept the provisions which I purpose to issue them." The issue of pork and flour was to be made by the agency traders, Galbraith said. "It is up to you now," he told them.

The action averted a crisis at the Upper Agency. At the Lower Agency, however, militant young Dakotas had formed a Soldiers' Lodge. Among other things their intention was to challenge the traders on their claims. They also argued for the immediate distribution of food. But the traders insisted that they would issue nothing until the cash annuities came. If the Indians were hungry, the trader Andrew J. Myrick said, "they can eat grass."

This statement lit the fuse and ignited Dakota anger that had been building for years and that now exploded at Acton Township on August 17, 1862. Four young Dakotas from the Rice Creek band on the Lower Agency had gone hunting for food. Unsuccessful in their hunt and returning to their Rice Creek village, one of them had come across eggs in the grass of a fencerow in front of a small frontier lodge and store. One of the Dakotas picked up the eggs for food. But a second warned him to leave the eggs alone. "They belong to a white man," he said.

The first became angry. "You are a coward," he charged. "You are afraid of the white man. You are afraid to take even an egg from him, though you are half-starved."

The second insisted that he was not a coward.

"You are a coward, and I will tell everybody so."

"I am *not* a coward. And I am not afraid of the white man." To prove it, he said, he would go inside the store and shoot the white man. "Are *you* brave enough to go with me?"

"I will go with you. And we will see who is the braver of the two."

All four of the men, bearing their shotguns, entered the store, and five settlers were shot and killed.

It was early evening when the four young Dakotas returned to their village on Rice Creek and explained that they had shot and killed five white settlers. A council of one hundred men from the Soldiers Lodge was immediately held to discuss what should be done.

Most of the men argued that once the killings were discovered, there would be bloody white retribution that would mean the elimination of all Indians in Minnesota. Before that happened, a full-scale war should be launched. Others argued that war against the whites was hopeless.

No, the first group insisted, a full-scale war could succeed because most of the white men in the state had gone off to the Civil War. Only boys and women remained.

But the white man was still everywhere. A war against him was foolish.

But even President Buchanan had warned that the traders were like rats who would try to steal Dakota land. A war now could drive the rats and all white men from the Minnesota River Valley. Sacred Dakota lands, which had been stolen by fraud, could be retaken.

Yes, Dakota lands had been stolen from them. But a war against white soldiers with cannons would be futile.

No, efforts to turn the Dakotas into "Dutchmen" and "cut-hairs" who struggled against the weather and infestations to till the soil and raise food — *that* was what was futile.

It was almost midnight when a decision was reached: the Dakotas would go to war. Of course, one hundred of them could do little, but they belonged to a nation eight thousand strong, in tiny and large Dakota bands scattered up and down the strip of reservation land. The one hundred needed to seek allies from those other bands in their effort to create an army of Dakotas that would sweep settlers from Dakota lands.

There was just one man in their nation who commanded the respect and experience to form that army. And it was after midnight when the one hundred men headed south in the night to his village.

3.

Little Crow

His name was Little Crow. As a boy he had attended a mission school, where he learned to read and write Dakota. Then he had left his father's village in Kaposia, near St. Paul, and headed west for the prairie, where he had married four sisters in succession and earned a reputation for card playing, gambling, and wildness. His father on his deathbed had urged his wayward son to give up his roistering and accept the responsibilities of becoming chief. But one of Little Crow's half brothers had contested the prodigal son's right to be chief, and with the entire tribe watching, the half brother had greeted Little Crow's return to the Kaposia village with shotgun in hand and told him to leave.

Little Crow had folded his arms over his chest as a sign of his defiance. "Shoot," he said, "where all can see. I am not afraid."

The eventual shot shattered Little Crow's forearms. A surgeon wanted to amputate his hands, but Little Crow refused to let him. The wounded forearms eventually healed, but for the rest of Little Crow's life, his wrists hung so crookedly that he hid them under a folded blanket at councils. As chief of his band he wore a headdress of weasel tails and buffalo horns, and he carried the dried skin of a crow as a talisman against evil.

Little Crow, with piercing hazel eyes, a long face, and a nose like the bill of a hawk had a face that suggested fiery intransigence, but he was described by whites as "suave," a shrewd diplomat, and a passionate orator who could never be cheated in discussions of his tribe's affairs. Still, in 1857 he had been a member of a party of Dakota chiefs who had gone to Washington and who in tall plug hats had looked oddly dignified as they agreed to accept further reservation confinement and ceded a ten-mile strip of reservation land to the U.S. government for a pittance.

Little Crow had at first objected. "You promised us we would have this land forever. Now you want to take half away."

Despite his objections, Little Crow had eventually signed the treaty with the other chiefs. Back at the two agencies, the young tribal hunters had considered the "Dutchman's" farming a futile solution to hunger. *Hunting* was the solution to starvation. Now Little Crow and the other chiefs had given up the only part of the reservation that had thick woods and plentiful game. It was nearly unforgivable.

The resentment over the ceding of land was still felt in June 1862 during an election for speaker for the entire Dakota nation. Little Crow was a candidate, along with Traveling Hail and Big Eagle, two other respected tribal chiefs from the Dakota nation. The title seemed logically Little Crow's because he was a passionate speaker and could argue forcefully. Additionally, he was a dignified figure with or without a plug hat. But Chief Traveling Hail was elected by an overwhelming majority. For Little Crow it was a bitter disappointment.

Still, Little Crow had shown bravery and tactical ingenuity

in battle. He was restless and full of energy. Once, guiding a party of mounted white men on an elk hunt, he had trotted alongside the hunters and chatted effortlessly for twenty-five miles each day of the hunt. It was the kind of inexhaustible vitality expected of battle chiefs. And it was he to whom the Dakota soldiers now turned for a leader, "shouting mad with enthusiasm."

Little Crow was fifty-two years old and sound asleep on the first floor of the two-story brick house the government had built for him at his village when the soldiers pounded on his door at dawn. Birds sounded cheerful wakeup calls. A little of the cold bite of fall was in the air.

Little Crow sat up in bed and rubbed the sleep from his eyes. He hardly seemed to be the spirited leader the warriors needed, but he carefully positioned his headdress while as many of the 150 members of the Lower Agency's Soldiers' Lodge as could crowded into his house and seated themselves. He listened carefully as they excitedly told the story of what had happened at Acton. His sixteen-year-old son, Wowinapa, stood behind him. The boy had a bony body and sad eyes, but he was braced like a stern sentry guarding over his father.

The soldiers finished by explaining that the white man would be coming soon to attack them. The Dakotas must act before that. Little Crow nodded. Yes, the white man would surely punish the Dakotas for the Acton murders.

But how could that be? the soldiers argued. All white men had gone off to war. The Great Father was even signing up half-breeds to fight. It was proof of how desperate the whites were for soldiers.

"Yes," Little Crow conceded, "they fight among themselves. But if you strike at them they will all turn on you and devour you and your women and your little children just as the locusts in their full time fall on the trees and devour all the leaves in one day."

Several of the soldiers raised their voices at once: before the whites could get help in Minnesota, the Dakotas would defeat them and have Dakota lands back. There would be abundant game and food again — buffalo, moose, deer, groves of sugar maple, and swamps with wild rice free for the taking.

By the time the warriors had finished arguing for war, several chiefs and head soldiers from other Lower Agency bands had arrived at the council. One of the chiefs took Little Crow's side. "War would be the act of a foolish child," he said. The nation should wait for the cash annuities and the issuance of food by the traders.

The cash annuities would never come, the warriors countered. And the traders were thieves. Now they needed Little Crow's advice and leadership in war.

It was a moment before Little Crow answered. "Last June you rejected me as your leader. Why do you come to me now for advice? Go to Traveling Hail," he said. "This war is not my work."

But Traveling Hail was a member of the "progressive white man's party." He was not the right man to lead the nation in battle against the white man.

"What comes from the mouths of those who want to fight," Traveling Hail interrupted, "is babble."

Little Crow turned for more support to a thirty-five-year-old chief whose village of thirty or forty warriors was close by Little Crow's. His name was Big Eagle, and his defeat along with Little Crow in the election for the prestigious role of the Dakota nation's speaker left the two leaders with a shared defeat. Big Eagle had a handsome face and a proud bearing and had sat for photographs showing him naked to the waist, his muscular chest bared, and holding a menacing knife as big as a scimitar across his lap. In those same pictures he wore six eagle feathers, representing the tribal enemies he had killed. The images suggested a warlike temperament, but he was a member of the Dakota Peace Party, and Little Crow considered him a "true chief."

Big Eagle spoke now in a steady, soft voice. "We might succeed for a time. But we will be overpowered at last and defeated."

Like Little Crow, Big Eagle had been a member of the delegation of Dakota chiefs who had gone to Washington and agreed to sell the strip of reservation land containing the last good hunting sites on the reservation. It was still considered an act of betrayal. And here he was, one of the betrayers, counseling peace!

Head warriors and other chiefs rose immediately to contradict Big Eagle. Better to die in a fight, the warriors insisted, than through starvation.

"If you had worked last season as farmers," another chief told them, "you would *not* be starving now."

Yes, the warriors admitted, the cut-hairs who had taken up the farming ways of the white man might have good crops and food. But more foul weather and pestilence would come, and the Dakota farmers would soon be hungry again.

If you choose to fight, Little Crow said, "you will die like the rabbits when the hungry wolves hunt them in the Hard Moon."

If that was so, then they were all doomed anyway. So why not fight to the end with glory?

"You are fools," Little Crow said. "Your eyes are full of smoke. Your ears are full of roaring waters. Braves, you are little children."

Red Middle Voice, chief of the militant Rice Creek band, sat in the front row of warriors wearing an imposing headdress. "Little Crow is a coward!" he said slowly.

Some of the warriors muttered their agreement.

Little Crow came to his feet quickly, beads of sweat on his forehead. He reached for Red Middle Voice's headdress and dashed it to the floor.

"Little Crow is not a coward!" he said. "And he is not a fool. When did he run away from his enemies?" Because the section of floor where he slept and now stood was elevated, Little Crow seemed to tower over Red Middle Voice, who offered only silence.

"When did Little Crow leave his braves behind him on the war path?"

He paused again. Still, there was silence from Red Middle Voice.

Now Little Crow spoke to all of them. "You are like little children. You don't know what you are doing. You are like dogs in the Hot Moon when they run mad and snap at their own shadows. We are only little herds of buffalo left scattered. The great herds that once covered the prairies are no more. See!" he said, his voice rising. Then he swept one of his blanketed arms to indicate the frontier. "The white men are like the locusts when they fly so thick the whole sky is a snowstorm. You may kill one, two, ten, but ten times ten will come to kill you. Count your fingers all day long, and white men with guns in their hands will come faster than you can count."

He sat back down. It was in part the logic of his own argument that they were all doomed that now helped convince him to lead the warriors. But he also realized that his leadership responsibilities could not be avoided.

His voice was soft but determined now. "Little Crow is *not* a coward," he said again. "He will die with you."

There was no turning away from the angry momentum of the warriors' arguments, and Big Eagle did an about-face as abrupt as Little Crow's.

"I will also lead you into war. We will act like brave Dakotas and do the best we can."

The Dakota women were the first to spring into action. While the soldiers cleaned their guns, the women ran bullets to small parties of warriors that quickly formed.

In Dakota villages up and down the Minnesota River, the Dakotas sang and danced and beat drums. Across the Minnesota River a small community of German settlers along Beaver Creek heard the distant commotion. "How plainly we hear the Indian drums," one of them remarked, unaware that the bellicose activity would soon be directed at the settlement.

Once the Dakotas were armed, a thousand men, wearing breech cloths, leggings, war sashes, and face paint, headed out across the prairie in small parties. The first casualties at the Lower Agency were the traders. Andrew Myrick, the trader who had said the Indians could eat grass if they were hungry, was quickly surrounded in his store, which was then set on fire. Myrick escaped out a back window, but he was run down, shot, and left to lie on the prairie with his mouth stuffed with grass. Clerks in the traders' stores were shot for being "dogs" who would not give the starving Dakotas credit.

Then the Dakota warriors turned their anger on the settlers. Those who could fled to St. Paul, Hastings, St. Cloud, New Ulm, and eastern Minnesota. Western Minnesota became nothing but "smoking ruins and deserted homes." Those who stayed behind gathered for safety in frontier villages and threw up hasty log stockades.

Warriors with shotguns and tomahawks chased down settlers trying to flee in ox carts. By midmorning hundreds of settlers, including women and children, had been killed. The worst incident was in that German community of settlers at Beaver Creek whose inhabitants had heard the distant Indian drums and gunfire. The unsuspecting settlers thought the gunfire was from Indians on the Lower Agency shooting at wild pigeons.

When Little Crow had learned of the killings of women and children, he spoke sternly. "Soldiers and young men," he said. "You ought not to kill women and children. You should have killed only those who have been robbing us for so long. Hereafter, make war in the manner of the white man."

The white man's manner of fighting meant that the Dakotas would soon be facing overwhelming forces. Little Crow could not expect to resist, or to prevail, with only a small army of soldiers from his village and the Lower Agency. He would need more soldiers, first from the villages in the Upper Agency. Then he needed to pick battle sites. The Dakotas needed to fight as villages and units and to coordinate their attacks.

The first encouraging victory for the Dakotas had been at a place called Redwood Ferry. There the Dakotas had ambushed and killed a party of forty-five militia men from Fort Ridgely. The party had been led by Captain John A. Marsh, who had fought in the First Battle of Bull Run. As soon as the first terrified settlers had begun arriving at Fort Ridgely, he had set out from the fort to investigate, despite warnings not to proceed into Dakota country with such a small force. Hiding in the bull rushes and bottomland thickets surrounding a ferry across the Minnesota River, the Dakotas had caught Captain Marsh and his men by surprise. Half of the men had been killed. Marsh himself had drowned in the Minnesota River trying to lead the rest to safety.

The victory at Redwood Ferry led to "wild torrents of exultation" among the Dakotas. They had proved that they could defeat the U.S. Army. On the Upper Agency news of the victory at the Redwood Ferry and the easy intimidation of frontier settlers led to a council of chiefs and head soldiers. They exchanged the same arguments and counterarguments for war. "You can easily enough kill a few white settlers," the cut-hairs said. "But the whole country will soon be filled with U.S. soldiers." It would be useless to fight.

No, others argued, they all stood in danger of being killed. So they should join the fighters on the Lower Agency immediately.

Dakota soldiers from the Upper Agency began arriving

at Little Crow's village, and soon approximately 250 teepees surrounded his brick house, which became Dakota battle headquarters. From there Little Crow laid plans to enlist the support of warriors from the Chippewa and Winnebago nations. The combined force of thousands of warriors would be sufficient to clear their ancient hunting grounds of white settlers. Warriors from the Winnebago nation would sweep down the Minnesota River from the prairie town of Mankato to St. Paul. The Chippewas, who were said to be eager to join the fight, would come down the Mississippi from northern Minnesota. Finally, the Dakotas led by Little Crow would come at St. Paul from the west. The powerful alliance of the three armies would then make a charge on Fort Snelling, the oldest military fort in the state, and overrun it. The ancient hunting grounds of Minnesota, which had been stolen by white settlers, would belong to the Dakotas again.

The first question for Little Crow and his fellow chiefs and head warriors to resolve was where first to attack. Wrapped in blankets, they sat up all night in Little Crow's house and argued possible courses of action. Some of the chiefs pointed out that terrified settlers were taking refuge in the frontier town of New Ulm, a settlement of nine hundred people with plenty of food and provisions. Overrunning the settlement would yield supplies that would help the Dakotas sustain the war effort. But again, there were counterarguments. One of the chiefs argued that if the Dakotas wanted to regain control of the entire Minnesota River Valley, that effort turned on control of Fort Ridgely. "If we take Fort Ridgely," the chief said, "nothing can stop us."

The fort consisted only of stone barracks, officers' quarters, a commissary, a headquarters building, stables, and a parade ground with a flagstaff. There were no ramparts or barricades, so the fort was less an impregnable fortress than it was a troop barracks that was vulnerable to attack from all quarters.

Little Crow had also favored attacking Fort Ridgely. But a critical issue was exactly how many soldiers were at the fort. Several parties of Dakota scouts were dispatched to crawl up to the fort under the cover of darkness and estimate the number of defenders. One of the parties came back with the news that they thought the fort was garrisoned by a mere forty soldiers. More troops were on their way, but for the time being, it meant a ten-to-one fighting advantage for the Dakotas. Battle success at Fort Ridgely seemed much more probable than trying to seize a frontier town of nearly a thousand.

Despite the scouts' report, the majority of the council voted to attack New Ulm, and on the afternoon of August 19, a small force of one hundred Dakotas without the leadership of Little Crow headed south for the town. The assault was short-lived. Although the New Ulm defenders, armed only with pitchforks and a few guns, huddled together in the barricaded town square like a "flock of sheep," the Dakotas could not penetrate the barricades, and without a battle leader to improvise and execute backup plans, the attack fizzled. Finally, a furious prairie thunderstorm swept over the town, and the Dakotas broke off the attack.

After the rain the weather turned muggy and hot. Meanwhile, that night at Fort Ridgely, dogs ran around the fort howling and yipping. Inside the refugee barracks, they could hear Dakota drums pounding in the distance. No one could sleep, and people lay wide awake, fearing an attack at any moment.

While the refugees tried to sleep, Little Crow laid plans for an attack at dawn. Four hundred warriors would assault the fort in four salients. The first attack, by a force of warriors under the command of Little Crow and meant to be diversionary, would come at the fort from the west side. Once Little Crow had created his diversion, three other salients would come at the garrison from the northeast, the east, and the south. The attackers would then set fire to the buildings, take the garrison and the refugees prisoner, and prepare for the next stage of the fight.

The signal for a coordinated attack was three rapid gunshots. The attack commenced with deafening gunfire and chilling war whoops. The Dakotas managed to set several of the fort's buildings on fire with flaming arrows, but just when the attack seemed about to succeed, the artillery detachments from among the defenders rolled their mountain howitzers into place. The artillery men quickly discovered that the cannons had been spiked with rags the night before, but it took only a moment for the soldiers to pick the rags out of the gun barrels, reload, and then fire into the attackers.

The effect was immediate, and the Dakotas scattered. Then another heavy rain fell; after three hours of battle Little Crow's men broke off their attack and retreated to Little Crow's village. That night more warriors from the Upper Agency arrived at Little Crow's encampment, and he laid plans for a second attack on Fort Ridgely with eight hundred warriors. This time there would be no diversionary attack. The Dakotas would encircle the fort, rush it from all sides, "and once again reign over the land stolen from us."

By Friday morning, August 22, Little Crow had moved his troops into position around the fort. Each warrior wore a sash in which he carried temporary food provisions to eat while fighting. Meanwhile, Little Crow had brought along young Dakota boys to make campfires in expectation of a long battle.

At three o'clock in the afternoon, the Dakotas began their attack. Little Crow had again directed that three shots be fired to commence the simultaneous charge. He gave strict orders that none of the warriors were to fire before the agreed-upon signal. But the arrival of the fort's mail carrier from the northeast corner drew three rapid shots from the Indians who saw him coming. The men on the south and west sides of the fort mistook the shots for the attack signal, and they began rushing the fort prematurely. They met stiff resistance, and their efforts to once more set buildings on fire with flaming arrows were ineffective because the rain of the night before had dampened the wood of the buildings.

Little Crow followed the action from an observation point on the brow of a hill northeast of the fort. From that position he passed word for his troops to mass at the southwest corner of the fort for a grand charge. Suddenly, a shell from one of the cannons positioned at the northeast corner of the fort whizzed by his ear. The crash of the shell just beyond him knocked him to the ground and stunned him. Afterward he would joke that he had seen the cannon ball coming and ducked, only to smash his head into a rock. However matters happened, subsequent reports were that the ball had grazed his chest, knocked him down, and fractured his skull.

Despite his injury, Little Crow watched as two mountain howitzers, all loaded with double canister, fired at once during the mass charge of Dakotas from the southwest corner. The echo of the larger twenty-four-pound howitzer echoed up and down the river valley. The canister balls tore holes in the ranks of the warriors. The fight was over. Inside the fort one of the defenders made a formal inspection of all the guard posts, serving whiskey to men who had been prepared to fight with their bayonets.

4.

Gray Bird

A LONE RIDER IN A SADDLE OF BEADED BUCKSKIN
had raced through the streets of St. Paul sounding the news
that out along the Minnesota River women and children by
the hundreds were being killed. "Governor Ramsey, Governor
Ramsey!" the rider shouted. "The Indians are at war and
killing all the white people." There were soon more alarming
reports. Fort Ridgely and New Ulm were under attack. The
whole western sky glowed with the fires of burning frontier
settlements and homesteads.

Citizen calls for action to "exterminate the savages," whose
nature was no more to be trusted than the wolf's, had been
immediate. Governor Ramsey telegraphed President Lincoln
and told him, "No one can conceive of the panic in the state."
Ramsey pleaded with Lincoln to postpone Minnesota's draft
allotment for the Civil War. The men were needed at home
to fight the Indians, Ramsey explained.

"Necessity knows no law," Lincoln responded. The

government could not postpone the draft. Meanwhile, Lincoln ordered Ramsey to "attend to the Indians!"

Ramsey had quickly picked Henry H. Sibley to command a frontier militia charged with putting down the uprising. Sibley was one of the most celebrated citizens of Minnesota. He had been described as the "black sheep" of his own family, and he had given up what he called the "irksome" study of law in favor of a more adventurous life on Mackinac Island as a clerk for a fur trading company. Eventually he had come to the upper Mississippi as an agent for the company, and he had helped create the Minnesota Territory. He had been a delegate to Congress, and in 1858 he had been elected the state's first governor. His fur trading business kept him in constant contact with Indians, who called him "Walker in the Pines." But after Governor Ramsey appointed him to end the frontier bloodshed, Sibley said his heart had hardened against the Dakotas "without any touch of mercy."

Sibley had never been to war or commanded troops. His militia was even less prepared. Ordinary citizens were encouraged to bring their own weapons and horses and join the militia. They were issued sky blue woolen trousers that were either too baggy or too tight. "My troops are entirely useless," Sibley complained publicly. They were undisciplined and untrained. They couldn't pitch a tent. They couldn't march or do close-order drill, and the pickets fell asleep at their posts.

On the day that Little Crow and his men made their first attack on Fort Ridgely, Sibley's militia of one thousand men had packed itself onto three decks of a steamboat and headed up the Minnesota River to St. Peter. Here he intended to properly train the men before going deeper into the dangerous frontier.

Sibley's reluctance to move, while news of more settler killings poured in, had brought criticism of him. In General George McClellan, the leader of Lincoln's Army of the

Potomac, the country had had enough of dilatory command-
ers, and in Minnesota the people turned on Sibley. "Sibley
the snail," they called him, "the state's undertaker." But Sibley
continued to refuse to move with such green troops, and
at St. Peter he stayed up all night checking picket posts to
make sure the men remained awake.

An additional problem was that the original issue of Belgian and Austrian rifles to Sibley's troops proved worthless.
The guns misfired or burst on discharge. Eventually, while
the militia was still at St. Peter, a small supply of better guns
arrived. These guns were rifled muskets made by Springfield, with a flip-up leaf sight and a triangular bayonet. But
the bullets carried in a rainbow trajectory, and so Sibley's
militiamen were advised to aim low.

It wasn't until August 28 that Sibley finally marched his
ragged troops to Fort Ridgely. Sibley's mule wagons, his
cavalry, and his militia made a column over a mile long that
snaked along the Minnesota River toward the fort. Stung
by the criticism of his snail's pace, Sibley led his troops in
a forced march for twenty-two miles before his weary men
reached Fort Ridgely, where he immediately assumed command. His first order was to send out the burial expedition.

Little Crow and two dozen of his best warriors sat in a tight
circle on the prairie around a steaming kettle of dog stew.
After the withering cannon fire at Fort Ridgely, the Dakotas
had retreated to Little Crow's village on the Lower Agency.
The next day, despite the lingering pain of his brush with
a cannon ball at Fort Ridgely, Little Crow led a final assault
on New Ulm. Again his warriors failed to capture the town.
But Little Crow left a dried crow's skin on the edge of the
battle as a mark that he had been there.

With rumors that Colonel Sibley was coming to fight
him, Little Crow led a five-mile-long column of three thousand Dakotas, some wearing settlers' gold watches on their

ankles, in a retreat farther north. The column included braying mules, barking dogs, some two hundred white and mixed-blood captives, including women and children, and Joe Coursolle's two daughters.

The column eventually stopped near a creek just north of the Upper Agency. From his noisy, bustling camp, Little Crow had taken his best soldiers out onto the open prairie, where they could hold a quiet council to discuss what to do next. On a crude flagstaff inside the circle, the U.S. flag fluttered in the prairie breeze. One by one in the circle of Little Crow's soldiers, each man spoke about how to continue the war.

For two weeks the Dakotas had been fighting steadily. They had moved dead tired in dusty columns back and forth across miles of prairie. They had retreated, then turned around to attack again. They had made rugged climbs up steep river bluffs. They had caught sleep and food whenever they could. They had fought through hard rains. They had buried their dead in prairie tombs. But there wasn't one of them that was ready to quit or surrender. And when each was done speaking in Little Crow's circle, he dipped a ladle into the kettle of dog stew and sat down to eat and wait for the next speaker.

Some spoke in favor of an eastward attack on the little frontier villages of Hutchinson and Forest City, arguing that the villages could be taken with ease. The Dakotas could also loot the abandoned towns and plunder the surrounding farms. Others argued in favor of moving a battle force back south along the Minnesota River to the towns of Mankato and St. Peter, which could be overrun and looted.

In the circle of warriors it was finally Little Crow's turn to speak. He pondered his situation before he spoke. His troops had fought four hard battles and failed to prevail in any of them — twice at Fort Ridgely and twice at New Ulm. What had once seemed easy gateways to Dakota control of the Minnesota River valley now seemed impregnable.

Little Crow's only success had been against the small

party of Captain Marsh's men at the Redwood Ferry. But the element of surprise that had led to that victory was gone. Wherever the Dakotas attacked now, the whites would meet them with frightening cannon fire whose buckshot whistled and hissed as it passed through their ranks.

Little Crow was convinced that he needed still more soldiers. But his hope that warriors from the Winnebago and Chippewa nations would join the fight had not been realized. And many of the Upper Agency Indians wanted no part of Little Crow's war or his encampment. "This is your affair," they had told him, "not ours!"

With so much disagreement over the war, two separate camps had been set up on either side of the creek, one promoting peace and the other, mostly made up of Little Crow's men, urging continued fighting. Little Crow and his men had immediately ridden across the creek to surround the peace camp and ordered them to join the combatants.

"We must form one camp together," Little Crow had said.

The peace camp had been adamant in their refusal, and Little Crow had gone back across the creek, vowing to return. But when he and his warriors returned, they were treated to a reconciliation feast by the peace camp. That spirit had prevailed until the peace camp insisted that Little Crow and his men give up their white captives.

The speaker for the Upper Agency was Little Crow's diminutive cousin, Paul Mazakutemani, called Little Paul, who was a gifted orator and a Christian convert. Little Paul said that his discovery of so many captive women and children had made his heart sad.

Wearing a collar shirt and a colorful scarf knotted at his throat, Little Paul had stood before a huge crowd of thousands of Dakotas from both camps. "Don't fight with women and children," he had begun. "Americans are a great people. They have lead, powder, guns. Stop fighting." Fighting with whites, he insisted, only led to "fleeing and starving."

Little Crow's warriors had leaped to their feet and objected. "If we die," one of them cried, "the captives die with us." Another had shouted, "We are men. As long as we live, we will not stop pointing guns at Americans."

Still a third Little Crow warrior had brought the argument to a close. "Don't mention the captives anymore!" he snapped.

Shouting and chanting, Little Crow and the men of his Soldiers' Lodge had mounted their ponies and returned to their camp. That night the Upper Agency Dakotas who opposed the war had formed their own Soldiers' Lodge, whose one hundred members had accompanied Little Paul across the creek to Little Crow's camp to insist on no more fighting.

"I have asked you to explain why you have made war on the white people," Little Paul began. "They have given us money, food, clothing, plows, powder, tobacco, guns. Why have you made war upon them?" he again demanded to know. Then he turned to Little Crow's warriors. "Those of you who do not wish to fight the white people, come over to me."

Little Paul's newly formed Soldiers' Lodge of one hundred men prepared to shield whatever renegades there were. But only a few came and stood with Little Paul.

Little Crow had insisted finally that they would not surrender like dogs. Once the white man had the Dakotas in their power, he said, every one of them would be hanged.

Little Paul had then changed his appeal. "Deliver me up the captives," he demanded. Stop the war!

Little Crow had answered that he had no intention of quitting the war or abandoning the great cause of reclaiming land. It was the Dakota birthright. But his tone was sad. And in his vow that he would never be taken alive, there had been defeat. If he were taken prisoner, he said, white people would display him like an animal in a cage. "No white man will touch me," he had vowed.

Sitting in the circle of his warriors around the kettle of dog stew, Little Crow's words came slowly. Both plans he had heard made sense. And after Little Crow spoke, the council eventually settled on a plan that represented a combination of the two battle tactics that had been discussed.

Half of Little Crow's men would proceed under the leadership of his head soldier Gray Bird, who had long been a member of Little Crow's band. By 1859 as more and more Dakotas accepted what seemed inevitable, Gray Bird had joined a farmer's band. Despite what might have seemed like the wrong temperament for a warrior, with the onset of the war Gray Bird had been picked by Little Crow to be the head soldier and speaker for the Soldiers' Lodge.

Now Little Crow directed Gray Bird to go southeast along the Minnesota River, skirt the impregnable fortress of Fort Ridgely with its powerful cannons and Sibley's troops, and cross the river to loot New Ulm, which had been abandoned. That same force then could move farther southeast along the river and simultaneously attack Mankato and the little settlement of St. Peter. Meager defenses in both towns meant a good chance for success. Or Gray Bird's band could improvise, and after looting New Ulm, it could go northwest to once more try and overrun Fort Ridgely. Finally, Gray Bird's warriors would attack St. Paul and "reduce it to ashes."

Meanwhile, Little Crow would lead a force of 150 of his warriors east. He and his men would thus protect Gray Bird's left flank and intercept any government forces on the way to the battlefront from Fort Snelling.

The next morning, Monday, September 1, Gray Bird and 340 Dakotas from various lodges, both warriors and women to do battlefield cooking, headed southeast along the Minnesota River. It was late afternoon when the Dakotas reached the Lower Agency and what had been Little Crow's village and headquarters. In the Dakotas' hurried evacuation of that camp, they had left behind supplies and property, and it was Gray Bird's intention to recover what he could.

But from the vantage point of the high river bluffs on which Little Crow's abandoned village sat, Dakota scouts looked across the river and spotted something astonishing. It was what looked like a column of mounted soldiers with wagons and teamsters "creeping across the prairie like so many ants."

Was it a detachment of Sibley's troops who had made bold to leave the protection of Fort Ridgely with its mighty canons and head out onto the prairie? And where exactly were they going?

It was sunset. Gray Bird consulted with the chiefs in his party and immediately sent five mounted scouts to race across the river and follow the column of creeping ants. It was dark when the scouts returned to Gray Bird's camp.

What was that column of ants, he wanted to know.

Just as suspected, they explained, it was a column of government troops.

How many men?

One company of mounted men—about seventy soldiers.

Where were they headed?

That wasn't clear. But it looked like they intended to make camp near the birch trees and trickling waters of Tanpa Yukon, or Birch Coulie!

With the surprise discovery of the encampment of soldiers beside Birch Coulie, the excitement of Gray Bird and his soldiers "knew no bounds." Gray Bird's force had moved southeast with the understanding that they would improvise on the battlefield as the situation demanded. Now here was an unexpected opportunity, more promising than the prospect of victories at Mankato, St. Peter, or Fort Ridgely. At Birch Coulie the Dakotas would have a clear superiority of forces, perhaps as much as two-to-one. The encampment was exposed and vulnerable, without the benefit of frightening artillery. Gray Bird and his troops could easily wipe out the entire detachment of seventy-five U.S. soldiers. Once they attacked, it would be over in minutes.

Dakota hopes for victory had been dashed at New Ulm and Fort Ridgely. Those defeats were exactly what those Dakotas who had argued against war had predicted. But here was a sudden, unexpected chance for victory that would be dramatic proof of Dakota power. The small force of soldiers at Birch Coulie could be wiped out. The defeat would prove costly for the white man, and his greedy designs on Indian land would have to be abandoned.

Gray Bird, with three other Dakota chiefs, quickly laid plans to surround with a force of two hundred warriors the Birch Coulie encampment under the cover of night. Gray Bird would lead Little Crow's soldiers around to the north side of the white soldiers' camp, approach at a crawl through the deep grass, and wait for dawn to attack. Chief Red Legs, the oldest of the chiefs at fifty-eight, would lead his band up the coulie from the river bottom and lie in wait on the east side of the encampment in the protection of the coulie. Chief Mankato, with the second-largest band in the Dakota nation, would split his forces. Half would station themselves with Red Legs's soldiers in the coulie, and the other half would lie in the deep grass to the south. Finally, Chief Big Eagle, with thirty men, would crawl through the deep grass to the west and then hide themselves behind the small knoll two hundred yards from the soldiers' encampment.

At the approach of dawn all four forces would attack at once. All would be bearing double-barreled shotguns loaded with buckshot and small round bullets called "traders balls" supplied by fur traders. There would surely be government sentries posted. But a few of the Dakotas would pass their muskets to fellow warriors in order to carry bows and arrows. Just before sunrise, with grass, golden rod, and ox-eyed daisies stuck in their headbands for camouflage, the bowmen would shoot the sentinels with silent arrows. Then the four bodies of Dakotas would attack in unison. Like an animal snare with deadly prongs, the trap would be sprung.

5.

Gaboo

Just before dawn at Birch Coulie, the wagons and picketed horses that had been silver in the moonlight began to turn gold. The expedition cook had been up since the middle of the night preparing breakfast for the troops. Captain Joe Anderson had instructed the cook to wake him if he heard anything suspicious. Now the cook noticed that the picketed horses were holding up their heads and seemed restless.

The cook crawled to Anderson's tent. "Get up, Captain." he whispered. "The camp is surrounded by Indians."

Anderson instructed the cook to quietly wake up the men. As the cook crawled from tent to tent, Private William Hart at one of the ten picket posts that Captain Grant had established the night before thought he spotted a dog or a wolf slinking through the deep grass. Hart's picket post was twenty yards out from the mouth of the horseshoe, between the encampment and the coulie, and he cautiously stepped closer to the suspicious movement in the grass, his musket at the ready.

Suddenly, a brightly painted Indian with a drawn bow rose from the grass. Hart raised his musket and fired. The shot broke the sunrise silence and echoed across the prairie.

For a moment Hart held his post and tried to pull a paper cartridge from his cartridge box, tear it open with his teeth, pour powder down the barrel, insert a Minié ball, push the bullet down the barrel with his ramrod, and get a percussion cap out of a cap pouch. It was then that he discovered Indians pouring up out of the coulie and sprinting straight at him. Twenty yards from him they began firing. Hart turned and ran for the safety of the encampment. Meanwhile, his fellow picket Private Richard Gibbons rose from the grass and fired. With no time to reload and fire his musket before the Indians were upon him, Gibbons turned and also fled for the encampment. But before he reached the mouth of the horseshoe, buckshot ripped through his back, and he fell.

From the coulie, from the deep grass to the north and west, and from the woods to the south, two hundred Indians rose at once and came at a zigzag run for the half circle of wagons. Their gunfire exploded from the four fronts of their attack as rapid and scattered as a string of deep firecrackers. From somewhere inside the wagons, a high hysterical voice broke over the gunfire: "Indians! Indians!"

Dakota bullets passed through the military tents at chest height. Inside one of the tents, a sergeant sprang to his feet and headed for the tent door. "Come on, boys," he shouted. "Don't be afraid."

Then a bullet struck him in the chest, and he fell. "I'm shot in the breast," he moaned.

Dakota war whoops filled the dawn. They shook blankets, waved flags, and beat drums. Five hundred yards to the west, Indian horsemen from Big Eagle's lodge raced back and forth. The impression for the surprised troops was that they were surrounded by a force of thousands.

Major Brown crawled from the officers' tent. Captain Grant followed him. In the dim light they could make out men bursting from the tents, half-dressed and still groggy with sleep.

Grant was the first to shout orders to the dazed men. But in the din and confusion the first troops out of the tents thought they had been directed to "fall in," and they stood line abreast for minutes in the center of the horseshoe as vulnerable as shooting-gallery targets.

Captain Anderson appeared suddenly and saw the men trying to form a line. "Goddamnit," he shouted, "lay on your bellies and shoot!"

In the hail of Indian fire thirty men who had tried to form a line lay dead or wounded. The survivors flopped to their bellies and began to return fire. But Captain Grant, eager to be sure that he had defenders at all compass points of his encampment, stood in front of the tents ordering the men who were still streaming out to "break left and right. Get behind the wagons and commence firing."

The most vulnerable spot for the encampment was the mouth of the horseshoe facing Birch Coulie, where the two pickets had first fired. At that moment Lieutenant Harry Gillham, a twenty-seven-year-old shavetail whom Captain Grant described as "fearless," ran from wagon to wagon, designating certain men to follow him. When he had selected a group of thirty men from behind the wagons, he shouted at them, "Follow me, boys!" and headed at a crouch for the vulnerable horseshoe opening facing the coulie. Meanwhile, most of the ninety-six horses picketed to the wagons had been shot, and Lieutenant Gillham ordered a handful of men to remain crouched while they dragged the carcasses of the dead animals to the mouth of the horseshoe, where the bodies could serve as breastworks. It was a maneuver that plugged the encampment's only opening, which the Indians were threatening to breach.

The first shots woke Private Bob Boyd out of a dead sleep in one of the tents. He sat up for a second to orient himself. Where was he? What the hell was happening? Around him men were already on their feet, belting their pants and grabbing their muskets. Boyd came to his knees and hooked his own belt in place. Then he reached for his musket with his left hand.

The bullet that struck him caught him just under his right eye, and he felt the right side of his face go numb. But the soldiers around him continued to rush from the tent, and Boyd struggled to his feet. He could hear Captain Grant shouting directions to the men. The vow Boyd had made earlier to give unquestioning obedience to Grant and to "fight regardless of danger . . . to the limit of my strength and endurance" was still fresh in his mind. Despite the bullet wound to his face, he joined the men running from the tent.

As soon as he was out the tent door, the man in front of him fell dead. "Lie low!" he heard Captain Grant shouting. "Lie low, all of you! Take good aim before you shoot!"

Boyd still had not fired one shot. He stood for a second, trying to decide behind which of the half circle of wagons to conceal himself.

In St. Charles Boyd had listened to thrilling stories brought back by a wounded Civil War veteran. Those stories had set Boyd's young mind afire with dreams of battlefield adventure. But this was the real, chilling thing, and bullets whizzed past him, then slapped through the tent canvas and turned it to lace.

Boyd had just started to move toward one of the wagons when a bullet tore through his right arm. Still on his feet, he tried to raise his musket to at least deliver a shot somewhere, but he found he couldn't raise the weapon. Blood ran down his right side, and a dull pain throbbed in his shoulder. When he finally looked to see where he had been wounded again, he found a large bullet hole in his shirt, just over his collar bone.

"Lie down," one of the soldiers who had followed him out of the tent shouted at him, "or you'll be shot again."

But he stubbornly remained on his feet and began running from one tent to another. Men already on their bellies finally tackled him to the ground and dragged him inside the officers' wall tent, which had been improvised to serve as a hospital tent and was already crowded with wounded.

Inside the tent Boyd sat up and pulled out a sharp pocket knife, which he opened with his teeth. Then he cut a hole in the canvas so that he could see out. Behind the wagons men were digging in the prairie, using pocket knives, bayonets, and mess pans to scoop shallow rifle pits and piling the dirt up for protection. The sight of his fellow soldiers fighting to the limits of *their* "strength and endurance" was more than he could lay idly watching, and he crawled from the hospital tent to join them.

He found the deep hole that had been dug the night before to cook the cattle meat. But as soon as he had crawled into the hole, those soldiers in the rifle pits beside him dragged him back into the tent a second time. Lying among the moaning wounded, he might have crawled out once more if he had not been struck by a third bullet, this one lodging deep in his right thigh. Two more bullets, spent from whatever they had passed through, fell harmlessly against his clothing. Finally, a shot horse fell onto the tent, and he had to struggle to be free of it. At that point he laid down again, resigned to his wounds and his fate.

Half of the men trapped in the encampment had taken up positions behind breastworks of wagons or horse carcasses. Some of them had even laid themselves out behind the bodies of their dead comrades. Still, there were pockets of panicked men who jumped to their feet to get a clearer view of the attacking Indians, and they were immediately shot. One young soldier ran behind the wagons shouting, "Oh, my God! Oh, my God!" He was tackled by one of the expedition's lieutenants, who pulled his revolver, cocked it, and warned the panicked soldier, "If you don't stop, I'll blow your brains out."

Major Brown continued to walk calmly among the men. The first bullet that struck him entered his back with a sickening thud. He fell and lay momentarily unconscious. Then he was up again, walking around, cheering on the men.

He stopped behind one of the wagons to encourage Private William Kathlow, who was lying in his rifle pit, to keep up a steady fire. But when Kathlow rose up to fire, a Dakota sharpshooter firing at him from behind a tree put a bullet through his shoulder. Kathlow rolled back as if dead. It brought the sharpshooter out from behind the tree. With Major Brown beside him, Kathlow popped up and put a bullet in the sharpshooter's head.

Major Brown stood up and began moving along the rifle pits again. Then a bullet struck him in the neck, and he fell immediately. Those men who saw him fall thought he had been shot through the heart. But he lay on the ground and continued to give directions. "Load and fire," he ordered, "but steady boys, steady, and give them hail Columbia."

In one of the rifle pits a fat recruit fought with another soldier for room. "God, bub," the recruit said, "I wish I was as little as you." Another of Grant's lieutenants, sprinting for a rifle pit, felt a thud against his chest that spun him around. Flattened to the ground, he discovered that it was his vest pocket watch that had saved him. Another soldier found that one of the musket balls had pierced his Bible, boring a clean hole that began in Genesis and didn't stop until halfway through Deuteronomy.

Behind the wagons other men worked so feverishly digging more rifle pits with their bayonets that the flesh on their hands turned raw and bloody. In one of the wagons, where she had lain since her rescue the day before, Justina Kreiger watched fearfully as one bullet after another tore through the canvas above her. Then a bullet knocked the cup from her hand as she tried to swallow medicine. On the west side of the encampment, facing the open prairie, a young half-blood who was part of the expedition's cavalry section suddenly left his musket behind and ran for the safety of the Dakota lines. He had hardly gotten out on the open prairie before Dakota fire killed him.

Elsewhere in the encampment, all but two of the ninety-six horses had been killed. One of the surviving horses belonged to Captain Grant, who crawled to the wagon where the horse was picketed and released it. The rest of the morning and afternoon, the stark white mount wandered and cantered through the spray of buckshot and bullets, seemingly oblivious to the surrounding mayhem.

After an hour's fighting, all of the military tents had been turned to lacework, but the Dakotas' initial attack had been checked. It was clear to the attackers that the encampment had more soldiers than their scouts had reported. It meant that hopes for a swift victory were gone. Withdrawn now to the safety of the woods, the coulie, or the deep grass, the Dakotas began desultory fire. The occasional bullets kept the men in the encampment flattened to their shallow rifle pits or huddled behind the horse carcasses. Those men who risked lifting their heads from their pits or over the riddled carcasses of the horses took bullets to the head and went immediately limp.

Some of the periodic Indian fire came from snipers in the Birch Coulie trees. From his firing position behind one of the wagons at the corner of the horseshoe, Joseph Coursolle spotted a sniper's barrel poking from the foliage of one of the coulie trees.

Before he had come to the Lower Agency with his family, Coursolle had run a trading post serving a small village of Indians on the southern Minnesota prairie. Among the Indians he was known as Gaboo. The name suggested that in name and heritage Joseph Coursolle, or Gaboo, was divided in his loyalties. But as he gripped his musket tightly and fixed on the spot from which the rifle poked from the trees, he had only one aim, which was not to miss.

At the crack of his shot a painted body slid through the branches of the tree and tumbled to the ground. Coursolle pulled his rifle back and crouched behind the wagon. "One less," he told the soldier who had taken up a position next to him.

But immediately a voice came from the coulie woods. "Hear me," the voice shouted at Coursolle. "We saw you shoot. You killed the son of Traveling Hail. Now we will kill your two little girls."

The idea that he had just shot the son of Traveling Hail, the revered speaker of the entire Dakota nation, meant little to Coursolle. Instead, his first thought was that his two young daughters were captives, and he shouted to no one in particular, "They're alive!"

Up to that point Coursolle had gone back and forth between the belief that they might still be hiding in the river bushes where he had left them, hungry and terrified, or the fear that they had been found by the Indians and killed. The news now that they had been taken captive by the Indians and were being held somewhere, probably still hungry and terrified, was hardly comforting. What if the Indian voice from the coulie meant what it said? Now the two little girls would die as retribution for Coursolle's deadly fire against the sniper.

But before he could dwell on that likelihood, a bullet struck the wagon wheel, and splinters flew in the face of the soldier next to him. His face plastered in the dirt, the soldier told Coursolle, "I was lucky that time." But a third man behind the wagon, who raised his head to see what had happened, toppled over dead with a bullet in his brain.

Then a voice from down the line of wagons rose. "This is my last cartridge!"

It was not a hopeless cry of defeat, but a call for additional ammunition from the backup supply of three thousand cartridges that had been loaded onto the wagon train at Fort Ridgely before it had set out. To some at the time the backup ammunition might have seemed like an unnecessary precaution since the expedition hadn't been heading out to a full-scale war that required much ammunition. Nor had the party expected to face a long siege by the warring Dakotas. Sure, the Dakotas fought among themselves—as nations and tribes and lodges—but they clearly had no appetite for the kind of stalemate warfare that white men were waging in the Civil War, with bloody battle lines, trenches, artillery bombardments, infantry charges, and the slow head-on collision of mighty armies.

To the soldiers of the burial party it was clear that what was going on up and down the Minnesota River was rampage and murder by small groups of "heathen" Indians, many of them probably fortified by alcohol. When it had finally sunk in what they had done, the Indians could be expected to hightail it west to safety in the wilderness. Meanwhile, the forty rounds of ammunition that each soldier had been assigned to carry gave the expedition enough firepower to confront the lawless bands and subdue them. It had seemed remote, the idea that the soldiers of the expedition would be surrounded and quickly exhaust their ammunition supplies. Now they needed to get at the wooden boxes of reserve ammunition to continue the fight. And the officers of the expedition ordered that the boxes be retrieved and the cartridges inside them distributed to the men.

Corporal Joseph Coursolle was one of the soldiers picked to do the work of retrieving the boxes. The men were directed to slide the boxes along behind the wagons for each soldier to replenish his supply. It would be dangerous work. But if that's what it took for the expedition to continue the fight, and eventually somehow rescue his two daughters, Coursolle was eager to help.

He crawled now on his back behind the line of wagons, squibbing himself along so that no more than inches of his body presented itself as a target. Once he had reached the ammunition wagon, he and several others positioned themselves under the wagon, raised their feet, and pushed it over. As it toppled and the wood crates slid to the ground, one of the men yowled from the pain of a bullet passing through his leg.

Next, Coursolle and the other men began sliding the boxes along behind the breastworks of wagons so that each man could help himself before sliding the boxes on. Once all the boxes of reserve ammunition had been distributed, Coursolle crawled back to his post, pleased over the ingenuity and success of the distribution.

It was then that one of the soldiers along the breastworks of wagons and dead horses shouted, "It's the wrong caliber!" The ordinance officer at Fort Ridgely had packed .62 caliber rather than .58 caliber ammunition. There was no point in any of the men remonstrating over the stupidity of the ordinance officer. With so many different muskets being utilized by the various frontier militias, he may have understandably figured they needed .62 caliber bullets. Whatever the reason there was only one thing to do now, which was for each soldier to take out his pocket knife or use the blade of his bayonet to swedge the lead bullets down to the right size.

It was tedious work. Flattened to the ground behind a wagon or huddled behind a horse carcass that occasionally shivered with an Indian shot, the men scraped away at the Minié balls. While they worked, another detail of men gathered up the rifles of the dead and wounded and redistributed them. It meant that each man along the defensive perimeter who was still alive and capable of firing had an extra loaded musket beside him, ready for whatever came.

All the men of the expedition expected at any moment a second Indian charge as frightening and hectic as the first.

The idea that they had an extra loaded musket beside them gave them little comfort. With nearly half of the expedition already out of action, if anything, they were less prepared to defend themselves. As the men waited, random shots from the attackers blew out wagon wood chips or sank into a horse carcass with the sound of a mattress being punched.

"Don't fire except when necessary!" one of the officers ordered.

Trying to pick another sniper out of the trees, like Joe Coursolle had done, or kill one of the concealed Indians as he moved in the woods or popped his head up out of the grass was only a waste of ammunition. When the Dakotas made their second charge, there would be plenty of clear targets to bring down. Meantime, the officers directed the men to stay low, work on shaving down the wrong-sized ammunition, and stay alert and on the ready.

Some of the men took powder from the wrong-sized cartridges and poured it down their gun barrels without a precious bullet. The subsequent gunfire, with an extra loud report, was meant to convince the Dakotas that the trapped soldiers still had plenty of firepower.

In the meantime the desperate cries for more ammunition had been met, even if that ammunition was the wrong size. But a midmorning sun was now beginning to bake the prairie, and the cries of "Water! Water!" went unmet. However convenient the cool stream of Birch Coulie might have seemed to Captain Grant when he chose the site, there was now no way to get to the water. And as the men exhausted the supplies in their canteens, more cries of "Water! Water!" rose from parched throats.

Inside the hospital tent Bob Boyd lay thirsty and unattended. The wounds in his face, shoulder, and leg had ceased burning, with each wound site having turned numb. An occasional Indian shot punctured the tent canvas and passed so close to his face that he felt the wind of the bullets. One of the expedition's teamsters crawled into the hospital tent and gave each wounded man a little raw cabbage, which they washed down with a sip of dishwater.

Outside the hospital tent, the men at the wagon breastworks could hear the Indians shouting directions to each other. It was obvious that they were moving men from one attack point to another in preparation for a second assault. Then the deep boom of cannon fire echoed over the encampment and across the prairie. None of the men dared to lift their heads to see from where the cannon reports were coming. Had the Indians during their frontier rampages taken Fort Ridgely and acquired the fort's cannons? Was this cannon fire the prelude to their expected second attack?

Bob Boyd listened to the cannon fire as more bullets cracked through the canvas with the sound of a sheet being snapped. He expected the Indians would breach the encampment and rush into the tent to kill him in hand-to-hand combat. He lay imagining half-naked, painted warriors flooding into the tent at any minute. His mind was clear, and he felt no fear, but he had no hope of escape.

Boyd slid the bayonet from his musket and lay as if he were dead, the weapon concealed in his good hand, his bloody face turned up to reinforce the appearance of death. His only thought was that he could perhaps kill one of his attackers before he was dead himself.

6.

Colonel Sam McPhail and Lieutenant Sheehan

FORT RIDGELY LAY SIXTEEN MILES SOUTHWEST of Birch Coulie. With his arrival at the fort, Colonel Sibley had positioned pickets around the fort to give advance warning of an attack. One of those Fort Ridgely pickets, stationed on a small hill twenty yards northwest of the fort, was nineteen-year-old Private Charles Watson, who had been recruited only two weeks earlier from Northfield, Minnesota. He was inexperienced and untrained, but he thought he heard distant gunfire from the northwest, intermingled with the prairie bird calls and the anvil strikes by the fort's blacksmith. Watson summoned Colonel Sibley to the hill and asked him to listen for the worrisome sounds.

Sibley said he heard nothing.

But didn't the colonel hear the distant gunfire?

Sibley cocked his head now and listened more intently. No, he repeated, he didn't hear it.

Sibley left, and Watson resumed the duties of his post. But the distant gunfire continued. It was clear to Watson now that it was coming from the direction in which the burial party, led by Captain Grant, had headed two days before.

Summoning the courage as a green private to again bother his commander, he called Colonel Sibley back to his picket post. The two of them stood quietly and listened. Then Sibley laid one ear to the ground in an effort to pick up the sound.

Once more Sibley insisted that he heard nothing unusual. Still, Watson seemed so certain of what he heard and from where it was coming that Sibley decided to take no chances. He ordered one of his experienced cavalrymen, a six-foot heavily bearded colonel named Sam McPhail, to take charge of a column of 240 men and head northwest on a reconnaissance mission to investigate the origins of the gunfire.

McPhail was a thirty-four-year-old Kentucky native who had distinguished himself in the Mexican War, during which he showed a fiery battlefield temper that had to bear the constraints of a squeaky voice. He had come to the Minnesota wilderness during the land boom to establish and map out frontier settlements. Indian skirmishes discouraged such settlements, he knew, and they had to be put down immediately.

Sibley's orders to McPhail were clear and brief. "You will ascertain the whereabouts of Major Brown's command," he ordered the colonel, "and you will relieve him if he is in trouble." His next orders would subsequently prove unwise. "You will move *cautiously*," he emphasized. "You will keep on the prairie as much as possible. You will avoid every possibility of an ambush."

Sibley also promised to have a six-pounder gun and a mountain howitzer catch up with McPhail as soon as the crews could be assembled. By noon McPhail and his column were moving northwest at a route step in a long column along the road to Fort Abercrombie, a military outpost far up the Minnesota River.

Many of the men were still recuperating from Sibley's

long forced march from St. Peter to Fort Ridgely. They complained that they were marching to Birch Coulie in their sleep. Eight miles out from Fort Ridgely, McPhail halted his column at a road fork.

While the men rested, McPhail waited for the promised six-pounder and mountain howitzer to catch up with him. Meanwhile, uncertain of the terrain ahead and, like Sibley, unable to distinguish the sound or location of gunfire, McPhail consulted with his lieutenants about which fork to take.

The left fork led to a deep ravine that McPhail worried in his squeaky voice might shelter Indians waiting to ambush him. In view of Sibley's stern directions to move cautiously, McPhail wanted to avoid the possibility of an ambush from the ravine, and he chose the right fork in the direction of Birch Coulie.

As soon as the six-pounder and the mountain howitzer arrived, the column moved out again. By midafternoon, McPhail's men approached Birch Coulie and fixed their binoculars on the encampment they could see through the trees. At first, they weren't sure if the pointed tents they spotted were military tents or teepees for a village of warring Indians.

McPhail sent two scouts on horseback forward toward Birch Coulie to investigate more closely. The scouts spotted the stars and stripes hanging limply in the stillness from an improvised flagpole at the center of the half circle of wagons. The bullet-riddled flag hanging over dead soldiers and horse carcasses seemed to signal defeat more than the courage it was meant to inspire.

Inside the horseshoe of Grant's wagons, the men watched as the two scouts rode their horses still closer to the coulie. Grant immediately ordered his men to fire shots to let the scouts and McPhail know they were still alive.

As the scouts approached the edge of the coulie, the Indians from Mankato's force turned about and fired on them, shooting their horses out from under them. The scouts retreated on foot back to McPhail. There they reported what they had seen. Grant was surrounded, cut off from water and food, and badly outnumbered. Birch Coulie itself was filled with Indians. There was no telling how many more were positioned at other points.

McPhail ordered his command to form a hollow square with the mounted men in front and the infantry holding both flanks. He had the six-pounder and the mountain howitzer positioned at the rear of the square, ready to come forward if needed. Once the square had been formed, McPhail ordered it to advance on the coulie.

From the deep coulie Mankato and his men watched the slow approach of the classic infantry square. As the square continued to move forward, Mankato quickly decided on just the kind of battlefield improvisation that had been discussed at Little Crow's council around the kettle of dog stew.

Fifty of Mankato's men, led by the chief, came up out of Birch Coulie at once in a long line, waving blankets and whooping and crossing paths as they charged. At the sight of Mankato's men, McPhail halted his advance and ordered the six-pounder and the howitzer forward in order to swing into action. They were loaded and laid and then fired at the line of Mankato's men, who broke immediately and retreated to the coulie.

Once they were certain that the cannon fire was friendly, the trapped men of Grant's expedition began cheering to celebrate their deliverance. Some of the men jumped to their feet and began to shout, "Hurrah! Hurrah!" Their voices drew immediate fire from the Indians, and the men dove back in their rifle pits for cover.

Despite the enthusiasm of the men, Major Brown woke up in the hospital tent, where he had been sleeping, and advised Grant to tell the men to remain watchful. "We are still in a bad fix," Brown said. Then he fell back asleep.

It was Brown's frontier experience speaking. The soldiers were still surrounded, they had the wrong ammunition for their muskets, they had no access to food or water, and they had lost half of their men in the first few minutes of combat. Additionally, the Indians were determined. Deliverance was *not* at hand, Brown knew.

The frightening tremolo of war whoops and cries continued to rise from Mankato's men and the Indians still in the coulie. The noise created the impression that thousands more Dakotas were poised to attack in a second wave. And practicing the caution that Sibley had ordered, McPhail halted his men and let his cannons fall silent.

The men inside the encampment realized what the sudden cannon silence meant. McPhail was retreating, and as suddenly as the trapped men had had their hopes for rescue raised, those hopes were dashed.

They began jeering and cursing McPhail, begging him to march on the coulie. But McPhail continued his retreat to a spot two miles east of Birch Coulie, where he instructed his men to dig rifle pits and prepare for an Indian ambush.

Mankato directed thirty of his soldiers to follow McPhail in retreat back across the prairie and then hide in the deep grass to keep up periodic fire against McPhail. Back in the coulie Mankato and the rest of his soldiers laughed and congratulated themselves on how effective their battlefield ploy had been.

Once McPhail's troops were dug in, and his cannons stationed in defensive positions, he put out a call to his men for a volunteer to ride back to Fort Ridgely with a message demanding reinforcements. The first volunteer was a twenty-five-year-old handsome Irish immigrant named Timothy J. Sheehan. Born in County Cork, Ireland, he had piercing blue eyes and a neatly trimmed mustache and beard. When he was two, both his parents had died; it made him, his friends said, "a self made man" who had emigrated to the United States at only fifteen. Eventually he had homesteaded a small plot of land outside Albert Lea, Minnesota, and taken up life as a bachelor farmer.

He had a powerful sense of dedication to his new country, and twice he had been elected as clerk for his township. That same sense of civic duty caused him to resign his clerk's position and enlist with the hopes of serving in the Civil War. But on October 11, 1861, he was mustered into the Fourth Minnesota Regiment, formed up to serve as "home guards" replacing the militia men who had gone off to the war.

That winter Private Sheehan and his regiment drilled daily at Fort Snelling in the frigid cold. Their mule teams sank in the snow and had to be pulled out by the men. Among a regiment whose members were green and untrained, Sheehan's self-reliance and discipline were spotted immediately by his superiors, and he was quickly promoted to corporal.

Three months later, Sheehan again caught the eye of his superiors, this time his regimental commander, and in February of 1862 he was promoted to first lieutenant in the Fifth Minnesota. He was assigned as a junior officer to Fort Ripley, a remote post on the Mississippi River in northern Minnesota where the most vigorous action by the troops was hunting and fishing. For Lieutenant Sheehan it was duty that promised little of the pride of serving on a Civil War battlefield.

Sheehan's first command on July 9, 1862, was to lead fifty men from Fort Ripley to the Upper Agency to maintain order while the annuities were distributed. He was next assigned to conduct a search for the infamous Inkpaduta, who had committed murder and mayhem in northern Iowa and southern Minnesota. Despite his failure to find Inkpaduta, young Lieutenant Sheehan was intrepid in his pursuit, and his military star continued to rise.

By mid-August Sheehan was leading his force of fifty men

in the long march from the Upper Agency back to Fort Ripley when he received the news that the Indians were killing settlers up and down the Minnesota River. Fort Ridgely, with only a handful of men to defend it, was in danger of being overrun. "We cannot hold out much longer," the fort's beleaguered troops warned. Sheehan and his men were ordered to force their march and return to Fort Ridgely to bolster defenses.

Sheehan led his command in a heroic march of over forty miles in nine hours. Some of the men trotted barefoot beside the wagons. Those who collapsed or couldn't keep up were permitted to ride in the wagons. Along the way of the forced march, Sheehan donned a red neck scarf to make sure his leadership was as conspicuous as possible.

When Sheehan arrived at Fort Ridgely, he learned that Captain Marsh, the fort's commanding officer, had drowned. It meant that just a year after his enlistment as a lowly private, the Irish recruit from County Cork, full of pluck but as green as shamrock, found himself temporarily the commanding officer of a major frontier fort.

Sheehan was the perfect volunteer to make the desperate ride from Birch Coulie to Fort Ridgely for help. He was eager to make what sacrifices he could for his new country. In his brief service as a soldier, he had shown his bravery repeatedly. He had proved he was energetic and resourceful. And he could follow orders.

The two men, McPhail and Sheehan, discussed what trail it would be safest for Sheehan to take in his ride to Fort Ridgely for reinforcements. The lieutenant could try to get to the south side of the Minnesota River and the Fort Ridgely trail, but crossing the river and the thicketed bottomland in broad daylight risked the same ambush that had led to the demise of Captain Marsh and his men. If he safely negotiated the river bottom, he could ascend to the prairie and then head southeast on the trail for Fort Ridgely. But once he was parallel to the fort, he would have to go back across the river again and risk a second ambush.

Alternatively, it was less than a half mile east to the Abercrombie Road, the same one McPhail and his men had just come up. The Abercrombie Road might be a shorter route, but it presented hazards of its own. It had begun as a crude Dakota trail along the north side of the river. Then ruts had been carved in the trail during a decade of travel by fur traders who used ox carts to transport their pelts to St. Paul. The Dakotas still continued using the trail, and it had been described as a "stretch of unprotected territory" that would be crawling with bloodthirsty Indians.

If Sheehan took the Abercrombie Road, he would have to slow down to negotiate the log causeways across cattail swamps and bogs. There would be boulders to dodge, along with roadside defiles from which an ambuscade could be sprung. There would be tight passages through shadowy groves. Across the open prairie, there would be tall Indian grass that could hide attackers.

Once Sheehan was mounted up, McPhail told him to head east for a half mile and then pick up the Fort Abercrombie Road. Once on the road, the lieutenant was to do his best to follow the wagon and mule cart ruts the sixteen miles to Fort Ridgely. At a full gallop he would be able to cover approximately ten miles in an hour. If Indians saw him in swift passage and tried to catch up to him, their weaker mounts fed only on prairie grass would not have the stamina to overtake him. If Sheehan were fired upon, McPhail told him, he was not to return fire or engage his attackers. He was to keep going at a gallop and outrun any pursuers. If all went well, without ambush or getting lost and with stopping once or twice to rest and water his horse, the lieutenant could make the ride to Fort Ridgely in approximately two hours.

Sheehan set out across the prairie, and McPhail watched

him disappear over a hill. Then the colonel heard shots, which he assumed were fired at Sheehan by Dakotas. It gave McPhail little hope that the lieutenant would survive a harrowing gauntlet of attacking Indians and make it back to Fort Ridgely.

The colonel turned to his men who had watched Sheehan disappear. Was there another volunteer? A boyish recruit from Rice County named William Wilkins stepped forward. He was ready to make the ride.

McPhail quickly rejected the bid. Wilkins was too young.

"Sir, I can make the ride!" Wilkins insisted.

McPhail recognized the young soldier's determination. "Boys," he shouted, "get me another mount and a saddle."

In minutes Wilkins had received the same directions as Sheehan, and McPhail lost sight of Wilkins galloping off in the direction of Fort Ridgely.

Meanwhile, Sheehan picked up the Abercrombie Road just beyond the shallow swale that marked the start of Birch Coulie. He was moving at a steady gallop down the road to Fort Ridgely when a shotgun sounded behind him. His horse bobbled and he had to steady him for several strides before the animal returned to a gallop. Then Sheehan checked behind him to see if he was being pursued.

He could not be sure how many Indian horsemen there were chasing him, but they were in a tight bunch in full pursuit. They fired at him repeatedly without closing ground on him but also without any of them dropping off. This was not the way it was supposed to go, Sheehan realized. His grain-fed mount, bred for stamina *and* speed, should have quickly left the Indian ponies far behind him.

After a half hour one by one the Indian pursuers dropped off until the road behind the lieutenant was empty. Sheehan stopped beside a tamarack swamp and dismounted to let his horse rest briefly and drink from the cool waters. Around him the prairie was silent, and the only sound he heard was that of his thirsty mount biting at the water and then chuffing between drinks.

While his horse drank, he checked the animal for wounds and spotted a red crease along the flank. Trickles of blood were flowing from the wound site. It was clearly the track of a bullet. But before Sheehan could investigate further, a shot sounded again. This time he heard the bullet strike his mount with a sickening thud. Sheehan prepared to find cover around the swamp. But the horse lifted his head and stepped sideways nervously, seemingly eager to get moving again.

Sheehan vaulted into the saddle and urged his wounded horse into a gallop. He was shortly moving once more at full speed. Just north of Fort Ridgely, a high ridge ran squarely across the Abercrombie Road. As soon as Sheehan accomplished the ridge, he could make out the buildings and smoke of Fort Ridgely. He spurred his mount on to an even faster gallop, and in one last sprint to the finish line, he flew past the pickets guarding the post against ambush.

Colonel Sibley, with a handful of his officers, met Sheehan on the parade ground of Fort Ridgely. Sheehan quickly dismounted, but before anybody could lead the gritty mount to the fort stables for water and grain, the animal dropped dead.

Then Sheehan presented Sibley with McPhail's message. "I have met the Indians," McPhail had written. "They are too much for us. Send reinforcements."

7.

Dr. Daniels

By nightfall the men inside Grant's encampment could make out campfires on the bluffs across the Minnesota River, where the Indians were gathered to enjoy a relaxing feast of cooked cattle captured earlier in the day and prepared by their women. If it were meant to tantalize Grant's hungry and thirsty troops, it served its purpose, and the trapped men watched with envy as the distant Indian figures moved like ghosts in the light of their campfires.

Grant and his men could hear the voices of the Indians celebrating their successes. The Dakotas had taken half the troops out of action while losing only three of their own warriors, whom they had buried wrapped in blankets in the soft soil of the coulie.

As the Dakotas relaxed and ate, they quarreled in loud voices. The issue was as old as warfare itself. Should they continue to surround the enemy stronghold, sit tight, and hold the noose around Grant's neck until he and his men surrendered from hunger and thirst? Or should they attack again at first light?

The Dakotas chose to attack again at dawn. In anticipation of that attack each of Grant's men readied the extra loaded musket beside him. A few of the mule drivers and teamsters with the expedition were positioned in the rifle pits beside the soldiers to load each rifle after it had been fired. For mule drivers, whose genius was knowing how to make mules behave, the task of loading muskets might have proved confusing. But it wasn't all that difficult: tear open a paper powder cartridge, pour the powder down the musket muzzle, and slip in the Minié ball, seating it with the ramrod. With proper coordination the preparation could cut the musket firing time significantly.

The men resolved not to fire before dawn. They periodically called "Wide awake!" to each other to encourage vigilance. The only additional sounds in the encampment came from the wounded men groaning in the hospital tent.

Captain Grant distributed a quarter of a hard cracker to each of his men, who tried to make jokes about their "heavy diet." To aid in washing down the dry crackers, they chewed bullets or pebbles to get their saliva flowing.

A heavy cloud cover moved over Birch Coulie and obscured the full moon. Some of the men cheered the prospect of rainfall, but the best the laboring heavens could produce was an electrical storm in the distance that shot jagged bolts of white to the earth.

Listening to the Indian voices, Grant rightly guessed that they were discussing strategy. Now that it was pitch dark—a night of "black despair," some of the men called it—Grant dispatched Louis Faribault, a half-blood scout who spoke perfect Dakota, to crawl through that dark to eavesdrop on the Indians and determine exactly what they were planning.

Faribault returned in an hour. "Captain," he told Grant, "I think you will have hard fighting in the morning."

Grant wanted an explanation.

"There are five hundred more Indians coming," Faribault told Grant. They were from the Upper Agency.

How could Faribault be sure?

The scout explained that he had gotten close enough to hear them talking around their cooking fires.

Before Faribault sprinted back to the encampment, he had shouted to the Dakotas, "You do very wrong to fire on us. We did not come to fight you. We only came out to bury the bodies of the whites you killed."

Unaware that Lieutenant Sheehan had already made a successful ride back to Fort Ridgely for help, Grant immediately decided that in view of Faribault's report the only chance for rescue of his trapped troops lay with themselves. He resolved then to send a man on horseback down Abercrombie Road to Fort Ridgely with an appeal for reinforcements. The only issues to be decided were who would make the ride and on which horse.

Grant instructed his men to crawl along the rope of picketed horses and select the sturdiest one. Apparently, Grant had forgotten just how deep his fix was because only two horses had survived the Dakotas' initial attack—Grant's white mount and another sturdy animal that remained on the picket rope.

During the heaviest fighting that day, Grant had released his horse from the picket rope, and the animal had wandered outside the encampment, feeding on prairie grass. At sunset the horse had wandered back into the encampment unscathed, and Grant had tried to put a halter on him. But the minute Grant stood up, he had drawn fire from the Indian snipers in the coulie.

"Down, Captain!" the men had shouted and then tackled him. It was action that had saved Grant, while his horse fell dead, riddled with bullet holes. The death of Grant's horse left just the one horse alive inside the circle of wagons, and at midnight men brought that last horse to Grant.

Corporal James Auge, a twenty-two-year-old French Canadian, volunteered to make the ride to Fort Ridgely. He was the expedition's leading interpreter, and since he knew Abercrombie Road and its landmarks, he stood in no danger of getting lost on the dark prairie. He had also lived among the Indians and was a friend of many. If the Dakotas intercepted him during his ride, there was a chance that he might be able to persuade them to let him pass.

Auge lifted one foot into a stirrup and took last-minute directions from Grant. The Dakotas had left overnight sentinels and snipers at the four points of their attack. Auge was to walk his mount quietly out the horseshoe entrance, then break into a gallop. Depending on the element of surprise, he was to squirt his mount through the opening between the Indian snipers to the north and to the east. Then, with his sturdy, grain-fed cavalry horse, once he was on the Abercrombie Road, he could simply outrun whatever Dakota horsemen took up the chase.

Once he got to Fort Ridgely, Auge was to tell the officers at the fort that Grant was surrounded and that the Indians were planning to attack in force at dawn. He was to make sure that Colonel Sibley understood the desperate situation of the burial party. Sibley was to immediately send as many reinforcements from the fort as he could spare. Auge assured Grant he would do as instructed.

Worried troops, convinced that Auge's ride would be their last chance for survival, watched as Auge swung himself into the saddle. Suddenly, flashes of heat lightning closer now to Birch Coulie illuminated Auge as he settled into the saddle. The sight of him spotlighted by lightening and ready to ride drew a volley of Indian fire. Auge leaped back out of the saddle and hugged the ground. Just beside him, the mount that would have brought rescue pranced and flinched as bullets struck him repeatedly. The horse fell dead.

Robert Boyd lay in the makeshift hospital tent drifting in and out of consciousness. Sometime after nightfall several of the half-bloods on the expedition dragged in a young private named Henry Rouleau, whose father was French and his mother Dakota. The half-bloods spoke to Rouleau briefly in French, reassuring him that he would survive, and then laid him beside Boyd.

Boyd could feel warm blood from Rouleau soaking into his own cap. "Where are you hurt?" Boyd managed to speak.

"Right in my head," Rouleau croaked. "I'll die now."

It reminded Boyd that his own head wound could be mortal.

Rouleau spoke in a whisper. "I never thought my mother's people would kill me."

Then a bullet crashed through Rouleau's hand. He cried out and suddenly went silent. In a half hour he was dead.

The wounded men were paired up and then brought drinking cups with a small portion of dishwater. "This is for you two," they were told. Each man took a sip and then passed the cup to his partner. The meager water rations led to the rumor among the wounded that the remaining healthy troops would try to make a night charge on the coulie to obtain fresh water. If they didn't do *something* to get water, the men around Boyd observed, it was certain death for them all.

"It's certain death whatever they do," someone else said.

Other wounded men with Boyd feared abandonment. Major Brown, drifting in and out of sleep in a corner of the tent, raised his head. "If we die," he said, "it will be defending you as well as ourselves."

It was almost midnight when Dr. Jared Daniels, the expedition's only battlefield surgeon, crawled into the makeshift hospital tent and began treating the wounded there. He carried with him a pocket surgical set, with a bone saw for amputation, a thin steel probe for investigating wounds, forceps for extracting bullets, a drill for penetrating the skull, and bandages and scissors.

Daniels's father had died in New Hampshire when he was four. He had been "bound out" as an indentured servant to a local farmer, and at eleven he had learned the trade of cabinet making. But his grandfather had been a surgeon in the War of 1812, and it wasn't long before Daniels left cabinet making to attend medical lectures at Bellevue College in New York.

With his medical degree in hand he came west in 1855 in the footsteps of his younger brother to become the first government physician for the Dakotas on the Upper Agency. He arrived just as the wild plum trees exploded with pink-red blossoms, and he fell in love with the prairie landscape. He married immediately and began serving the Dakotas, treating their ailments and binding wounds they received in periodic battles with the Chippewas.

Daniels was described by his white friends as a "gentleman of the old school," but he was very much at home among the Dakotas. As the agency physician he took up modest quarters with his wife and children in the attic room of the agency's blacksmith shop. He learned to speak Dakota, and he sympathized with their reservation troubles. He loved to watch their women dance to fiddle music, "like in any city in the country," he said. He had himself danced with Indian women who wore ribbon anklets and colorful dresses. Dakota men came to his small medical quarters on the agency and sat sharing the news from other villages as if they were cracker-barrel philosophers in a country store. "We are very much attached to Dr. Daniels," they said.

Then the call came for surgeons in the Civil War. The army told him that most of his training and expertise in battlefield surgery could be learned on the job. But he studied graphic battlefield reports from surgeons sawing off shattered limbs or drilling to find buried bullets. To him the work seemed only a variation of the sawing and drilling he had once done as a cabinet maker. Additionally, he had the experience of fixing the wounds suffered by Dakota warriors. In any case, there would be no exacting licensing boards to face, only a few questions from an army exam board, and then he would be ready for duty.

He was appointed assistant surgeon for Minnesota's Sixth Regiment. His first assignment was treating the wounded after the attack on New Ulm. In a hotel converted to serve as a hospital, Daniels worked alongside a five-foot-four Englishman named Charles Mayo treating the injured.

Then he had been picked by Major Brown to accompany the burial expedition into Dakota Country. At Birch Coulie those very same Dakotas who had been his patients and were attached to him were now shooting at him. But he had left his medical studies with the Hippocratic Oath imprinted on his mind. "Whatever house I may visit," that oath said in part, "I will come for the benefit of the sick." It didn't matter who was shooting at him or why. If he had been trapped in an encampment of his Dakota friends who needed medical help and the situation were reversed so that it was his white friends who were shooting at him, he would have done his utmost to save whomever he could. That was what he was trying to do at Birch Coulie, save lives. If any of the wounded died, it wouldn't be because he hadn't tried to save them.

Once inside the hospital tent, which was illuminated by soft lamplight, Daniels lifted his head and spotted Major Brown still drifting in and out of sleep in the corner of the tent. The doctor examined and dressed the wounds in Brown's back and neck.

The lamplit tent was like a beacon in the night that drew steady Dakota fire, and bullets continued to slap against the canvas walls of the makeshift hospital. Daniels told Brown that he would be safer in one of the rifle pits dug by the men.

As Brown crawled out, one of the wounded men shouted, "We shall all be scalped!" Before he disappeared in the night,

Brown shouted back, with all the determination he could muster from his wounded body, "No, we won't!"

Daniels looked around the hospital for his next patient. Several of them were lifeless and gray, by all indications dead. Then he spotted Boyd and crawled to him. Boyd's leg wound had stopped bleeding and was not life threatening. The bullet crease through the flesh just beneath his eye was not as bad as it looked.

Daniels turned his attention to Boyd's shoulder wound. Slow-moving large-caliber round balls created gaping holes in victims. The ball in Boyd's shoulder had left a huge puncture and shattered his collar bone. Daniels first probed the wound with one finger, looking for bone fragments or the ball. There were pieces of bone everywhere in the shoulder, and Daniels took his grasping forceps and began picking them out one by one.

Daniels looked at his patient, whose eyes were closed. "Does this hurt?" he asked.

"A little bit," Boyd answered. But Boyd was now drawing on the resources for overlooking pain that he had learned as a boy when he invited playground friends to stick him with pins.

Daniels worked propped on one elbow so that he could see into Boyd's wound. As he was taking out the last of the bone fragments with his grasping forceps, a volley of bullets tore through the tent. Daniels slammed himself facedown onto the tent floor. More moans rose from the other wounded men in the tent.

The shooting stopped as suddenly as it had begun, and Daniels propped himself on one elbow again. He bound Boyd's wound with a gauze wrap and moved on to the next soldier.

8.

The Messenger

WITH MCPHAIL'S CAUTIOUS TROOPS PULLED BACK, there was now little hope by the men of the burial expedition of rescue. The silence of the night was punctuated by cries from the wounded for water and food. Despite the overcast skies and the heat lightning, it did not rain, and the men sipped dishwater in an effort to slake their thirst, which had been aggravated in the act of biting powder cartridges to double-load their muskets. All during the night they were instructed again and again not to fire their weapons before the expected attack at dawn.

Back at Fort Ridgely Sibley's militia men, still recovering from the twenty-two-mile forced march to the fort only days before, had just sat down to a light supper when Lieutenant Sheehan brought the news of the Birch Coulie disaster. Sibley organized a relief expedition of a thousand men to leave immediately. The men were each given two pieces of hard bread. By 6:00 p.m., they were in line for another long march, this time sixteen miles through the dead of night to Birch Coulie.

At midnight Colonel Sibley's relief column from Fort Ridgely reached McPhail's campsite three miles east of Birch Coulie. If Sibley reprimanded McPhail for the latter's extraordinary caution, it was not recorded anywhere. Instead, confident that the Indians would wait until dawn to launch their attack, Sibley told the men to get a good night's sleep. After two long and tiring forced marches, the men dropped onto the prairie grass and immediately fell dead asleep.

The Dakota warriors continued to come and go from their posts in order to eat at their campfires while the head soldiers laid their battle plans for dawn. In the attack of the day before, the Dakotas had come at the encampment in four separate salients. Inside the encampment Grant and Brown had countered by moving soldiers from one side to the other as the pressure points changed. It had been a tactic that had helped save the day for the white soldiers. This time the Dakotas resolved initially to retain the north, south, east, and west divisions of their troops, but then they would merge the warriors into a continuous force of attackers, mounted and on foot, who would circle and circle in an ever-tightening noose. It was a tactic that would preserve the mystery of where the final penetration would come. It would come from *everywhere*. In the end the Dakotas would sweep through the breastworks and be inside the encampment.

But before they attacked and wiped out the remaining soldiers, they resolved to offer safe passage to the half-bloods among Grant's men. Having killed whites and mixed-bloods indiscriminately, having dismissed "cut-hairs" and "breeches Indians" as turncoats, Dakota motives for offering safe passage to Grant's half-bloods were murky. Indeed, the absence during the discussion of some of the chiefs who remained at their battle stations or retired to eat made the decision appear to lack consensus. Still, in the minds of some of the Dakota leaders, who were guilty of the same caution that had stopped McPhail in his tracks, Dakota superiority was marginal since only a few more soldiers from the Upper Agency had joined the Indian forces at Birch Coulie that night. It thus made sense to try to remove nearly a dozen of the enemy from inside the Birch Coulie breastworks in one stroke before the final attack.

It was the most spectacular sunrise many of the white soldiers had ever seen. It began as just a dim glow that seemed to come out of the trees of Birch Coulie, suggesting that the coulie itself was the origin of all light. Then the glow lifted itself above the trees like a rose-colored fog. Finally, there it was: the bright, paper-thin, blood-red circle of the sun.

At 5:00 a.m., in the first dim light of that rising sun, Captain Grant and his men could just make out the Dakotas stretched in a long line that moved like a snake constricting silently around the camp. Suddenly, the line of Dakotas began whooping as they moved, half-dancing, half-marching.

The men who had been drifting in and out of sleep in their rifle pits were wide awake now. Each man grabbed his musket, laid it on the dirt parapet of his rifle pit, and prepared to fire.

Then Grant's voice broke in the quiet. "Hold your fire!"

From the deep grass to the north, where Gray Bird's men had been concentrated, an Indian messenger carrying a white flag of truce approached the encampment on a white pony that would not come head-on toward the circled wagons but canted left and then right as if the horse and rider were all part of an uncertain proposition. The rider wore a breech cloth and a war shirt with leather trappings, and he waved the truce flag vigorously. One hundred yards from the encampment of Grant's men, he stopped.

Again, Grant turned to Corporal James Auge for help. "Find out what he wants," Grant said. Auge walked out unarmed to the edge of the deep grass.

"We have reinforced ourselves during the night," the messenger began. "Now we are as many as the leaves on the trees. We are going to make a charge and kill all the men in your camp. You cannot resist. We will kill every soldier." He paused before he continued. "But we do not want to kill our Dakota brothers. If the half-breeds march out and give up, they will be protected." He paused again to look to the line of soldiers beyond Auge. "All in camp who have Dakota blood, come out. We will not harm you."

The messenger waited while Auge turned around and translated the offer to Grant and the men who had gathered about him, some with loaded muskets. Grant spoke now to the half-bloods, who had understood the offer and stood as a group close to Grant. "What do you fellows intend to do?" Grant asked.

Half of them spoke no English, and so they waited for Auge to interpret Grant's question.

"You are free to go," Grant said. "Each man can make his choice."

The half-bloods were left alone to talk among themselves in Dakota. They could all claim Indian heritage. Mixed-bloods, some called them. It was quite different from the term "half-breeds," which suggested they contained two separate and disconnected halves, one Indian, one white. The truth was that they were each a mixture of moods and convictions that made a whole new alloy that set them apart.

Led by Auge, a dozen of them stood in a close circle and talked quietly. One by one they sorted through their uncertainties: was the offer of safe passage for them legitimate, or would they be shot as soon as they reached Dakota lines? With the encampment reduced by a dozen men, would it give an even greater numerical advantage to the attackers? But if their attackers weren't bluffing and they really were "as many as the leaves on the trees," what difference would twelve fewer men make? The Dakotas already had an overwhelming superiority.

Auge turned finally to Gaboo. "What do you say?" he asked. Did Gaboo think reconciliation for the half-bloods was possible? Was the offer of mercy and safe passage legitimate?

It was an easy decision for Joe Coursolle. Yes, he was half-Indian through his mother. And he had been fully accepted when living among the Dakotas on the Lower Agency. But all that mattered was that in the Birch Coulie battle, Gaboo had shot Traveling Hail's son, and Mankato's men in the coulie had shouted vows to kill him and his daughters.

"If I go," Gaboo answered, "Traveling Hail's band will chop me up like pemmican meat." Mercy and reconciliation were not possible. "I will stay," he told Auge.

When the men were done conferring, Grant wanted to know what they intended to do. Auge spoke for them all in perfect English. "We want nothing to do with these Indians," he said and pointed to the coulie and the grass out of which the messenger with the white flag had come. "We will stand by you and fight as long as there is a man left."

Emboldened by the support of the half-bloods, Grant instructed Auge to tell the messenger, "All the Indians who want to die should come at once. We have two hundred fighting men with plenty of ammunition."

Auge walked back out to the edge of the grass and delivered Grant's final message. Then Auge added threats of his own. "We are just like white men," he said on behalf of the mixed-bloods in the encampment. "We all came here to fight." Made cocksure by Grant's threats and exaggerations, Auge shouted, "If you think you can whip us, what makes you stay so far away?" The messenger waited for Auge to finish.

"Come fight us," Auge said. "You don't have enough men to take our camp." Auge repeated Grant's exaggeration. "We still have two hundred men. Each man has five muskets loaded."

In truth there were only sixty-five men left in the encampment who could resist another assault. And each had only two muskets, not five. But Grant's and Auge's falsehoods were no worse than the messenger's contention that the Dakotas were now as "many as the leaves on the trees."

"All the Indians who want to die should come at once," Auge finished. "Little Crow can not take us. You do not dare fight like soldiers. You kill women and children. You fight like Chippewas. Go back and stay with your squaws." Auge stepped toward the mounted messenger and spit at the feet of his horse.

While Grant had not been able to follow the exchange between Auge and the messenger, it was clear that Auge had spoken defiantly. Now Grant followed in the same tone. "Tell him to get out of the way," Grant instructed Auge. "I cannot respect a flag of truce."

Auge barked Grant's new directions at the messenger.

"He's to go at once!" Grant repeated. But the messenger retreated at the same unhurried pace as his advance.

Grant turned to the soldiers beside him. "Fire!" he ordered.

Half the men raised their muskets and fired. The white horse fell and the messenger had to struggle to keep from getting his legs pinned beneath the mount. But once he was on his feet, he disappeared at a sprint into the tall grass.

Grant had directed his men to fire on the bearer of a white flag of truce. For the Dakotas it was villainous, and their plans for a coordinated attack dissolved in an instant of fury and mayhem. Warriors on horseback began circling closer and closer to the encampment.

"Hold your fire," Grant shouted to his men back in their rifle pits. "Lay low, until they are close upon us."

The Indians continued to circle, closer and closer.

"Take good aim and fire!" Grant ordered now. "Seize the other gun and repeat."

This time the cannon fire that stopped the Dakota attack was from Sibley's relief force. The fire was close by and the canister whistling through the coulie leaves made a crackling sound. It sent the Dakotas back to their original positions.

In their rifle pits some of the men lifted their heads and spotted the glimmer of polished bayonets in the distance. A few of them jumped up to welcome this new prospect of relief. But with the arrival of McPhail's column the day before, the men had already celebrated their relief prematurely. Grant wasn't going to let them do it again. "Stay at your posts," Grant barked at the men. "Watch for Indians."

Then a large, powerful-looking Dakota appeared out of the coulie woods. He began waving a yellow blanket and shouting direction to the rest of Mankato's men in the woods to the south.

Grant brought Corporal Auge to his side again. "What's he saying?"

"He says three miles of white men are coming."

Grant tried to focus his gaze through the coulie woods in the direction from which McPhail had come. If it was McPhail's cannons sounding again, there was every likelihood that he would be turned back once more by a Dakota counterattack.

But Sibley had awakened his men at dawn, told them to forget breakfast, and formed them in a skirmish line. He had put portions of his thousand-man force on his flanks for protection. Then he had rolled his cannons forward and ordered the detachments to rip canister through the coulie trees.

Initially Dakota forces from the four attack positions had rushed across the coulie and gathered for a counterattack. But they did not stand long in the face of the canister fire before they turned back to the safety of the coulie. They left a few snipers behind at each of their attack positions to protect their retreat. Then they worked their way down the coulie toward its confluence with the Minnesota River.

Having watched the Indian forces disappear back in the coulie, Sibley moved his troops farther up the ravine, crossed at one of its shallower points, and then moved on the encampment from the northeast. When the colonel marched his troops into the horseshoe of wagons at 11:00 a.m., the high sun was just beginning to burn the dew off the dead men and horses. Some of the dead horses had swelled in the hot sun and burst, spilling their entrails onto the grass like tangles of purple rope. The stench made the rescuers gag. Of the original complement of 153 men, 23 were dead or dying, and 60 were wounded. Over half of the party that had set out to bury the prairie dead had themselves become casualties. One of those was Thomas J. Galbraith, the Indian agent who had helped stoke Dakota anger. The wounds he suffered in the Birch Coulie fight, however grave, seemed less than he deserved for his intransigence.

A few of the men cheered. Most groaned, begged for food and water, or cried. Joe Coursolle stood bolt erect but crying, dreading that he would have to tell his wife that he had failed to find his two daughters. As Sibley shook hands with the survivors who could stand, others complained quietly that he should have come to their relief sooner. They were quick to tell him that despite the emergency swedging of cartridges they had done, they had almost run out of ammunition.

Men too weak or wounded to lift themselves out of their rifle pits made sure that Sibley saw the splintered remains of the tipped wagons that had helped save them. They also showed him one tent with so many holes in it that its canvas sagged from the center pole like tattered lace. Major Joe Brown pointed out to Sibley 140 holes in the hospital tent, where he had drifted in and out of sleep.

Among the wounded was Private Robert K. Boyd, who managed to get to his feet, stumble out of the hospital tent, and greet Sibley and his rescuers. He had a bullet gash across his cheek wide enough to lay his thumb in. His right eye was swollen shut. His right arm and hand were swollen to twice their normal size and hung useless by his side. His face was covered with blood and dirt, and fellow soldiers from his regiment who had rescued him had no idea who he was.

"Boys," he shouted, "did ya never see me before?"

9.

Little Paul

LITTLE CROW RODE EAST ACROSS THE PRAIRIE IN THE box of a horse-drawn wagon whose axles creaked and grunted. Following the battle plan agreed to over the kettle of dog stew, he was leading an expedition of 110 Dakotas who would try to block the route of government reinforcements headed for Fort Ridgely. At the same time his head soldier, Gray Bird, had been picked to lead the effort to overrun Mankato and St. Peter.

It was a plan to which Little Crow had given his blessings. But there had been repeated Indian defeats at New Ulm and Fort Ridgely. And only a few Upper Agency Dakotas had joined the war effort. It left Little Crow without the huge army he knew he needed to defeat Sibley. Additionally, Gray Bird had been deflected from his part of the mission by the sudden opportunity to wipe out Grant's troops at Birch Coulie.

That opportunity at Birch Coulie had ended in a standoff. For Little Crow the conclusion was inescapable. It was time to make peace, and as he bounced along in the wagon, he set to work composing in his head a note to Sibley and Governor Ramsey. His hope was that they would agree to peace terms rather than the annihilation that Little Crow's soldiers had grimly argued was inevitable. Little Crow's note to Ramsey and Sibley proposed a cessation of hostilities and then a treaty. Perhaps, the Dakota leader hoped, a treaty could be drawn up without provisions for all of the Dakota soldiers to be hanged.

Little Crow and his men made camp that night on the prairie. His soldiers listened carefully as he read the note that he had composed for Governor Ramsey and Sibley. When he was done reading, the men hooted and jeered his idea of a peace overture. Some of his men threatened to kill him. His soldiers were not ready to give up on a war they had been so ardent about fighting, and Little Crow quickly tore up the note.

The next morning seventy-five of Little Crow's men refused to follow the reluctant general any farther east to set up the blockade. It left Little Crow with just thirty-five men willing to accept his leadership. There was no point any longer in pretending that he was the battle leader Dakota warriors had wanted the night they woke him up from a dead sleep. Instead, he was just another Dakota soldier in a fight that already seemed lost, and he turned over his command to one of his half brothers and rode quietly in the wagon that creaked and grunted across the prairie.

Before Colonel Sibley departed the Birch Coulie battlefield, he had a detail of men temporarily bury the dead. When that was done, he fed Grant's hungry troops a meal of pork, flour cakes fried in the pork fat, and coffee. The tents were struck, and the wounded men were loaded moaning and wheezing into ambulance wagons. Finally, unaware that Little Crow had not fought at Birch Coulie and had already entertained the idea of a truce, Sibley left a note for the chief in a cigar box tied to a stake which he drove into the ground. The note demanded to know why the war had been started. "If Little Crow has anything to say," Sibley wrote, "send a flag of truce." Then Sibley led a long column that left Birch Coulie and headed back toward Fort Ridgely.

By the time Little Crow got the note, he had returned to the Upper Agency. He immediately responded to the note, saying that the war had started because the government had not lived up to its treaty promises. He wrote, "We made a treaty with the government but have to beg for what we get, and we can't get that until our children are dying." Little Crow went on to warn that he was holding many captives, women and children. There was no mistaking the implications: they could be used as bargaining chips for peace.

Sibley answered quickly. He reminded the chief that Little Crow and his men had already killed hundreds of settlers. Release the captives, he told Little Crow, and then they could talk "man to man."

Whatever overtures for peace that Little Crow had originally entertained were now gone. And it was clear to Little Crow, the Dakota chiefs, and the people in their villages that Sibley with his force of over a thousand soldiers would soon be coming after them.

Criers came through the camp and called for all the Dakota villages to strike their tents. They left the next morning in a five-mile-long column of Dakotas and captives that moved north for safety. But as soon as the column was about to reach the Chippewa River, it was stopped by Red Iron, the same headstrong chief who after the treaty at Traverse des Sioux had vowed that he could never be broken by white men. He was as unyielding now with Little Crow and his column. They could not pass.

"You commenced the outbreak," Red Iron told him. "You must do the fighting in your own country."

That night Little Crow and his captives made a separate camp from the Upper Agency Dakotas. In Little Crow's "hostile" camp the Dakotas danced and sang and boasted of what they had done on the battlefield. In the camp of the "friendlies," the Dakotas wanted nothing more to do with the war, and they called for the immediate release of all captives. The subsequent arguments between the two camps lasted for days and were fierce.

"Their agents and traders have robbed and cheated us," one of the hostiles argued. "Some of our people have been shot, some hanged . . . and many have been starved. The matter has gone too far to be remedied. We have got to die . . . let the prisoners die with us."

The belligerence was answered by Little Paul Mazakutemani, the gifted orator who had earlier tried to persuade Little Crow to release the captives. Little Paul was so short he had to mount a barrel top now to hold command over the two quarreling camps. "The Americans have given us money, food, clothing, ploughs, powder, tobacco, guns, knives. . . . Why have you made war on the white people?" he asked the hostiles to explain. There was no answer from the audience.

"I am opposed to continuing this war," Little Paul continued, "or of committing further outrages. Give me all these white captives. I will deliver them up to their friends."

"If we are to die," the answer came, "these captives shall die with us."

"In fighting whites," Little Paul insisted, "you are fighting lightning and thunder. Deliver up to me the captives. And as many of you as don't wish to fight with the whites, gather yourselves together and come to me."

"We shall die bravely," the hostiles answered. "Don't mention the captives anymore."

The friendlies then demanded that all the hostages be taken to Fort Ridgely and turned over to the soldiers there.

No! They should all be massacred!

The quarrel between the two camps turned violent. Gunfire was exchanged, tomahawks brandished. Meanwhile, rumors began circulating that Little Crow had issued orders for the captives to be killed.

The truth was that he was continuing to despair over his lost leadership, and the plans for peace he had once torn up were now back on his mind. He sent another note to Sibley. In this note he reminded the colonel that he was still holding 150 prisoners. "I want to know from you as a friend," he said, "in what way I can make peace for my people."

It had been a seesaw war. But the failure of the Dakotas to prevail at Fort Ridgely and New Ulm and finally at the Battle of Birch Coulie gave Sibley the upper hand. His answer to Little Crow's offer was firm: before there were any more discussions of peace, Sibley wanted the prisoners returned under a flag of truce. Not until then would he negotiate peace terms.

Back at Fort Ridgely Sibley made provisions to use his overwhelming military force against the Dakotas in order to secure a flag of truce and the release of the captives. But because additional green militiamen poured into Fort Ridgely to supplement Sibley's army, his preparations to go after Little Crow went slowly.

All the new troops were ill prepared for hard battle, Sibley felt. The answer was close-order drill from dawn to dusk on the parade grounds of Fort Ridgely. Sibley's drill sergeants tried to follow the Army's field drill instructions that were supposed to be an instrument for troop discipline and fighting readiness. But once the men were assembled on the parade ground and read the instructions for "wheeling by file," they were utterly confused.

"If the wheel be to the side of the rear rank," the drill sergeants read, "the front rank man will wheel in the step of twenty-eight inches." The instruction led to a rat's nest of bewildered, shuffling troops and drill sergeants hollering to restore order.

Meanwhile, Sibley continued to put off marching until still more troops arrived. When his army reached two thousand men, some of the troops joked about "Sibley the snail," who had enough men now to defeat Robert E. Lee.

There was also irritation expressed in St. Paul newspapers over "Sibley the State undertaker" and his slow pace. His response was to write Governor Ramsey and offer his resignation. The offer was refused.

For Joseph Coursolle the wait and the postponement of the rescue his own two daughters was maddening. He dared to hope that Elizabeth and Minnie were still alive. And he was eager to march for a second rescue attempt. But Sibley's column would be marching up Fort Abercrombie Road and passing within the stench of Birch Coulie, where prairie crows were hard at work picking clean the bones of the dead horses. If the wind was right as Sibley's column passed, the soldiers would be able to pick up the smell of the Birch Coulie battlefield. It would stand as a reminder to Coursolle of how close he had come himself to annihilation.

The question now was whether or not Sibley's expedition north to chase down Little Crow and secure the release of the captives would also face annihilation. No matter how big Sibley's army grew, would Coursolle wind up surrounded again, frustrated once more in his efforts to be reunited with his daughters?

Sibley finally moved out from Fort Ridgely with 1,400 men on September 19. The troops, cavalry, artillery detachments, and supply wagons made a column along Fort Abercrombie Road that stretched as far as the eye could see. But each new day's march wasn't started until midmorning. Then Sibley stopped the column at noon for a midday meal. Finally, he went into camp each day at 4:00 p.m., so the men would have time to dig rifle pits and construct barricades in case of attack.

Coursolle and his fellow soldiers cursed Sibley. They could be "crawling on their bellies" and make better time, they joked. St. Paul newspapers picked up the theme of Sibley's slowness and wrote that he was moving his troops with "the dignified leisure of a commissary train."

Four days after setting out Sibley's column made camp just south of the Yellow Medicine River at a place called Wood Lake only miles from the separate encampments of the friendlies and hostiles. It had been devastating cannon fire with withering canister that had repeatedly repulsed Indian attacks. Now the presence of an artillery detachment gave Sibley confidence that he could employ cannons again to achieve the same frightening effect, scattering to the winds whatever Indian forces he faced.

As soon as Sibley's expedition made camp, Little Crow sent scouts to determine the surrounding terrain and Sibley's troop deployment. The scouts reported to Little Crow that Sibley had artillery and had thrown up defensive breastworks that would be difficult to assault. At a council of head soldiers and chiefs, Little Crow proposed a nighttime surprise attack on Sibley's encampment from all quarters, with a stampede of the expedition's horses and mules. But Little Crow's battle authority was almost gone now, and others argued that an attack under the cover of darkness lacked courage. The council settled on a surprise attack at first light when Sibley's column broke camp and resumed its march northward.

That night criers moved through the two Indian camps, ordering the men to prepare to fight Sibley at dawn. "All must fight," the criers called. The attack would be on the front and rear of Sibley's column, with secondary assaults pinching the column until it was cut in two like a long centipede. Then the two parts would be squashed. The six hundred warriors who went off to the fight before dawn told themselves, "We will have plenty of hardtack and pork tonight." Never mind what had happened at Fort Ridgely and New Ulm or Birch Coulie. This time they would prevail. The result would be annihilation of Sibley's troops.

Instead, the result for the Dakotas was disaster. A detachment of Sibley's troops sent out at dawn to forage corn and vegetables nearly drove their wagons over Indian troops hidden in the prairie grass. Having lost the element of surprise, Little Crow's men attacked but were turned away. A nearly spent cannon ball from Sibley's artillery still had enough power to kill Chief Mankato, whose brilliant deception at Birch Coulie had stopped Colonel McPhail. Armed with only a six-shooter, Little Crow watched with dismay from a nearby hill as the disaster unfolded. After the defeat, Dakota warriors returned to their camp in small disorderly groups.

"I am ashamed to call myself Dakota," a nearly heartbroken Little Crow said. Seven hundred handpicked warriors had been defeated by cowardly whites! "Better run away and scatter over the plains like buffalo and wolves."

After finally agreeing to the release of the captives, Little Crow and one hundred Dakota warriors fled west, first to Big Stone Lake, then Devil's Lake. As he made his escape from the certain vengeance of the white man, Little Crow looked back on land that had belonged to his ancestors as long as time. The dream of recapturing that land was gone. "We shall never go back there," he said.

After the victory at Wood Lake Colonel Sibley ordered his troops to perform a two-hour dress parade on the prairie. The action showcased only for the benefit of the grass the close-order drill maneuvers the men had tried so hard to learn on the Fort Ridgely parade grounds.

As the men marched, there were conflicting rumors

everywhere among the troops about the fate of the captives. They had all been killed. No, they had all been taken west by the hostiles. But the captives were still alive! For Joe Coursolle, so close to learning the fate of his two daughters, Sibley's dress parade was inexcusable, and the corporal muttered angry curses against the colonel at the risk of court-martial

Still, Colonel Sibley waited three more days before moving north to the camp where the captives were gathered waiting release. The bayonets of the troops twinkled in the sunlight as they marched into what became known as Camp Release. Friendly Indian drums and white flags greeted them. Little Paul, who had argued so vehemently with the hostiles for release of the captives, greeted Sibley.

"This is good work we do today," he told the colonel.

Half-starved and some naked, 270 captives, including over 100 white women and children, ran toward Sibley's column when it arrived. Joe Coursolle spotted his two daughters in a group of women and children sprinting toward the column. Coursolle threw down his heavy musket, broke from the ranks, and ran to meet his daughters.

"Papa, Papa!" Elizabeth shouted as Coursolle grabbed hold of her. Minnie also leaped toward him and clutched one of his legs.

The girls were covered with dirt. The dresses they had been wearing when they had hid in the river thickets almost a month earlier were now tattered and torn. But they were alive.

The government's ruse for seizing the Dakota warriors who had participated in the outbreak was ingenious. The Dakotas were told to appear at the Upper Agency warehouse and form a line to receive the overdue annuity payments. Two clerks sat at a table taking a conspicuous and "official" roll. After each Indian was counted, the men were separated from the women with the explanation that the men were entitled to an *additional* annuity. Once they were isolated, 234 Dakota men were arrested.

A five-man military commission held trials at Camp Release and later in a rude log house on the Lower Agency. The first man to appear was a "mulatto" named Godfrey, who had been at the Battle of Birch Coulie and was sentenced to be hanged. However, after his sentence was commuted, he immediately turned state's evidence. His subsequent testimony against other Dakotas was tainted by his commutation, but it was instrumental in the conviction of others.

The commission heard the evidence against 392 Dakota men. There were no lawyers and no provision for the appearance of defense witnesses. As a result of the hearings, 307 Dakotas who admitted to having taken part in any of the various battles, including the Battle of Birch Coulie, were sentenced to be hanged in Mankato, Minnesota.

The condemned prisoners were moved in a long column to Mankato to await their fate. Along the way the citizens of New Ulm, determined to take justice into their own hands, attacked the column and had to be repulsed by Sibley's men.

In the meantime, there were calls from some quarters to "lay the blame for this great crime where it belongs, with the atrocious Indian system." Critics described the arrangement as an "organized system of robbery." And the white man was enjoying luxuries and wealth "over the bones of these poor fellows."

Minnesota officials responsible for administering justice began to have second thoughts about their authority to execute 307 Indians. Among those sentenced was Little Thunder, who was charged with murdering one of the Coursolle daughters even though she had survived, and there were pleas from some quarters for officials to reconsider the guilt of the condemned. The argument was that the guilty

Indians had all fled with Little Crow. Those condemned now to be hanged had turned themselves in. If they were guilty, why would they have turned themselves in, violating the law of "self preservation"? Weren't the condemned prisoners who had admitted only to being at the Battle of Birch Coulie combatants entitled to the rights of soldiers instead of criminals to be executed? Wouldn't the whole world view the execution of three hundred enemy soldiers as a barbaric violation of the rules of warfare?

In the fall of 1862 Minnesota officials passed the execution decision along to President Lincoln. The president appointed two lawyers to review each case and assign death sentences to only those Dakotas who were guilty of wanton murder or rape as opposed to accepted soldierly conduct of war. The two lawyers cleared all but thirty-nine Dakotas, who were sentenced to hang. As the day of execution approached, Lincoln granted a reprieve to one of the condemned.

For the condemned a huge square wooden scaffold was constructed in the center of Mankato to serve for a public hanging. The execution was set for December 26, 1862.

A bitter cold snap hit Minnesota in early December 1862. It brought sharp winds and subzero temperatures. Then it turned almost balmy, with heavy rains that left bare ground and thick mud. The newspapers lamented that there was not even enough snow for sleighing. Without the snow there would be no "Christmas merry bells."

Still, it was not a silent Christmas in Mankato, and thousands of citizens cheered when the scaffold dropped and thirty-eight Dakota Indians were hanged at once. Among them were men whose only crime had been that they had fought as resolute Dakota soldiers at the Battle of Birch Coulie.

It was a summer evening in Minnesota in early July 1863. In western Minnesota, to which many of the panicked settlers still had not returned, preparations were underway to celebrate the nation's eighty-eighth anniversary. There had been no rain in June in Minnesota, and the Mississippi was described as a "respectable creek." Forest fires on the north shore of Lake Superior left a pall of smoke over the state that blocked out the sun. The whole state seemed on fire, and citizens complained of eating and drinking smoke.

Chief Little Crow, architect for the Dakota battle plans, had been on the run for ten months. He moved from Minnesota west to the James River, a "paradise for the buffalo hunter," to Devil's Lake, where he had failed in his efforts to recruit members of the Gros Ventre and Mandan nations to join him in raids on Minnesota in the spring.

Little Crow had finally retreated north to Canada. But now, with a small party of sixteen men from his lodge, including his son Wowinapa, he had returned to smoky Minnesota to steal horses for the welfare of his other children. But the citizens of the state were still angry over the conduct of the Dakotas, especially that of the elusive Little Crow. The guilty leaders of the uprising were still being sought out, captured, tried, and hanged. Forced to avoid capture and traveling mainly at night, in Minnesota Little Crow and his party were soon starving.

On the evening of July 3, Little Crow and Wowinapa discovered a wild raspberry patch in a copse of trees near the town of Hutchinson. What little sun was visible through the smoke was just setting, leaving behind a soft streak of pink the length of the horizon. The berry patch was suffused with a serenity and calm. Feeling no imminent danger, Little Crow and Wowinapa laid down the guns they were both carrying and began eagerly picking and consuming the berries.

Suddenly Nathan Lampson and his son, Chauncey, two Hutchinson residents hunting deer in the same area, spotted Little Crow and Wowinapa. Lampson and his son had no idea who the Indians were or what they had done, but recent murders and thefts in the area were suspected to be the work of Dakotas still hiding out from the war, and Nathan and Chauncey were immediately on guard.

The two deer hunters were father and son, as were the two berry pickers. But otherwise they were profoundly separated by the enmity of their two nations, and the standoff between them was brief.

The father Nathan Lampson leveled his gun and fired at the father Little Crow from behind a poplar tree. The bullet struck Little Crow in the hip but was not mortal. The Dakota leader quickly reached for his son Wowinapa's gun and fired back, grazing Lampson in the shoulder. Then Little Crow picked up and fired his own gun. At the same instant the son Chauncey Lampson fired at Little Crow. The ball glanced off the stock of Little Crow's weapon and entered his chest.

"I am killed," Little Crow moaned, then dropped to the ground.

Wowinapa tried to comfort his father, who lay on his back beside the raspberry bushes. Little Crow managed to lift his head to whisper, "You have to go on alone."

Wowinapa dressed his father's feet with new moccasins and covered him with blankets and leaves. He folded Little Crow's crooked arms over his body. Finally, he laid out a coat to make a pillow for his father's head. Then Wowinapa fled, leaving his mortally wounded father lying beside the raspberry patch, Little Crow's improbable dream of the return of ancestral lands finally crushed. By the time Little Crow was dead, it was pitch dark.

10.

Epilogues

EIGHTY-FIVE-YEAR-OLD ROBERT K. BOYD STOOD ON a makeshift wood stage beside Birch Coulie. It was Labor Day 1930, and a crowd of thousands had gathered to remember the Battle of Birch Coulie. The air, which sixty-eight years earlier had been filled with the stench of dead soldiers and horse carcasses, now smelled of freshly plowed sod. Dust from arriving cars drifted from the gravel roads like fire smoke. The music of meadowlarks filled the pauses between tunes of a big brass band.

Many in the huge crowd were settlers who had come west as part of a second land boom that included Minnesota and that had been no different than the first. "Free land," promoters had advertised, "open for settlers." It was described as the "new El Dorado . . . Eden . . . Nile's garden." And it had all been cleared of Indians. Settlers flocked to the "land of opportunity" to homestead 160-acre farms. Then drought and the Depression popped the bubble again.

Not a few of those "boomers" in the huge crowd faced

mortgage foreclosures and the hard times of the Depression. They had been drawn to the festivities partly on the advertised promise that two large corn-fed steers would be barbequed and served as a lunch for forty cents a plate.

Additionally, the Indian chief Zat Sam would be there to perform his lasso acts and tricks of ventriloquism. Parachutists would jump from a biplane at high altitude. There would be footraces, mounted horses, and covered wagons. Finally, full-blooded Sioux Indians would be on hand to participate in a reenactment of the Battle of Birch Coulie.

Robert K. Boyd was the featured speaker and attraction because he was the least likely survivor of the battle. After the fight he had lain in various Minnesota hospitals for nearly a year, surrounded by Civil War wounded who fought surgical fevers and suffered pyremia and gangrene. Most of them died. Nurses dressed Boyd's three wounds daily, but the wounds still drained pus, and he spiked a fever. He was incoherent for weeks and clung to life only on the strength of his conviction that he had been prepared to survive the ordeal because his playground friends had agreed to stick knives and pins in him.

He received a disability discharge from the army in March 1863 and began limping through life with a Birch Coulie bullet still in his leg and a shoulder that ached from the bones that had been shattered. And he watched with interest as characters more important than he had been at Birch Coulie, and much less wounded, fell one by one.

Little Crow was dead, his body dragged from its shallow grave by dogs. Firecrackers were stuffed in his ears and nose, and then he was beheaded.

For Gray Bird, Little Crow's deputy and one of the leaders at the Battle of Birch Coulie, the prospect of facing the same horrible fate as Little Crow was unthinkable, and he simply disappeared after the battle. Newspaper speculation was that he and the other battle leaders and warriors had fled west with Little Crow to the Red River Valley and then probably to Canada. Wherever he had gone, Gray Bird had never faced trial, and his name had never appeared on the annuity rolls. He had vanished.

Chief Red Iron had defied the government's efforts to "break him" as a chief. He had been equally defiant in refusing Little Crow passage through his land. After the uprising was put down, he helped minister to the condemned Dakota prisoners in Mankato. Then he became a scout for the army's expeditions into western Sioux lands. As a reward for his services, he was given a tract of land on a bucolic lake west of Sisseton, South Dakota, where he lived with his family until his death in 1884. He was buried in a grave overlooking the lake he had come to love. Eventually the lake site became a resort for rich white tourists. But even in death the stalwart chief who had insisted that his Indian power was too great to ever be broken kept his sovereignty, and the resort took the name Red Iron Lake.

After peace and order were restored to Minnesota, Little Paul, who had argued so forcefully against the war and for release of the hostages, became a scout for recently promoted General Sibley's expedition of 1863 into Indian Territory. The expedition moved from Minnesota to Big Stone Lake on the border with the Dakotas, then across the Sheyenne River, and finally all the way to the mighty Missouri River. For his services as a scout the government awarded Little Paul five hundred dollars. "I have regarded myself as a white man," he said. His statement stood as his heartfelt expression of the path of peace and Christianity he had chosen. His name was inscribed by grateful white men on a prairie monument. In 1880 his reminiscences were published and reflected the part he had played in trying to bring peace. He died on the Sisseton Reservation in South Dakota in 1886.

Despite criticism leveled at him for moving at a snail's pace in the campaign against the Dakotas, Henry H. Sibley was promoted to brigadier general. At the head of what had once been a ragtag army, he and his soldiers helped gain control of those western counties of Minnesota that had been abandoned during the conflict. Then he led the expedition of 1863 to pursue the "hostiles" west into the high prairie of Indian country, where no white man except hunters and trappers had ever set foot.

In old age he was acclaimed for his "distinguished" and "meritorious" military leadership during the Dakota War. He had the honor of serving as a congressman from the territory, and then he was elected as the state's first governor.

But newspaper criticism stung him. Editors called him blundering and incompetent. By his sixties he looked haggard, and his face had darkened, as if the responsibilities and strains of his active life had worn him down. Shortly before his death he tried to sum up his life. "I have been thinking about my life," he said, "and have decided that it is well nigh a failure." He died in February 1891 without specifying what he thought those failures had been.

After the Battle of Birch Coulie, Joseph "Gaboo" Coursolle also accompanied General Sibley as a scout on the expedition into Indian Territory. Eventually Coursolle took his family to the Santee Reservation in Nebraska, where he raised eight children, including Elizabeth and Minnie, whose rescue he had helped achieve. But for the rest of his life Coursolle would never forget that brief discussion at Birch Coulie over whether or not to accept the Dakota offers of amnesty for the half-bloods. It was a moment during which the two parts of his life, Indian and white, collided with a thunderclap.

Coursolle would also never forget that night after the first Dakota attack at Birch Coulie. It had been the longest night of his life, he said. And the things that had happened were too horrible to describe.

Yet he gave a dramatic oral history of his part in the Dakota War to his son, who passed the account along until it was eventually recorded. When Coursolle died in the 1890s, no other participant in the Battle of Birch Coulie, other than Robert K. Boyd, had written or spoken more about the battle than Joseph "Gaboo" Coursolle.

For almost thirty years Captain Hiram P. Grant offered no official account of what had happened to him and his men at Birch Coulie. Instead, he went off to the Civil War with the Sixth Minnesota Regiment and rose to the rank of lieutenant colonel. Eventually Grant explained that his silence was because he *had* written a detailed report immediately after the battle, but he had been told by his superiors at Fort Ridgely to submit his report to Major Brown, who had been in command of the expedition.

"This was the first I had heard of it," Grant said. "To say that I was angry would express only half of what I felt." He ripped up his report and never submitted it.

"If any blame rests upon any one for selection of camps or carrying out any details of the expedition, it rests upon *me*," he insisted.

There was no doubt in Robert K. Boyd's mind about who had been in charge. It had been Captain Grant, who had noticed the young private's earnest work at grave digging and had given Boyd the first compliment of his life. And when Boyd heard the news in 1897 that yet another notable survivor of the Birch Coulie battle had died, he was especially saddened by the loss.

After the captives had been released at Wood Lake, Chief Big Eagle surrendered to Minnesota authorities on what he said was good faith. He was a prisoner of war, he felt, and should be treated accordingly. He had not murdered anyone. "If I had killed or wounded a man, it had been in an open, fair fight." Still, he was tried by the military commission and sentenced to hang. He protested again that he had not done anything to deserve execution. His sentence was eventually commuted, and he spent four years in the federal prison in Davenport, Iowa.

After his release from prison Big Eagle lived for forty years on a farm outside Granite Falls, Minnesota, not far from Birch Coulie. He took the name "Jerome" and converted to Christianity. In June 1894 he gave a newspaper reporter the only Dakota account of the war that included the Battle of Birch Coulie. In stirring detail he described how he and his thirty men, waiting to attack that first morning, had hidden in the deep grass behind a small knoll two hundred yards west of the horseshoe of soldiers. His account of Dakota War strategies and tactics, from one of the few who would have known what those tactics were, should have stood as reliable. But after his story was published in a St. Paul newspaper, whites called Big Eagle "Big Liar" and accused him of numerous inaccuracies.

"My white neighbors and friends," he answered that criticism, "know my character as a citizen and a man."

Not long before he died in 1906, the once fierce-looking warrior who had sat for a photograph of himself stripped to the waist, wearing eagle feathers and bearing a long and murderous-looking knife, now looked serene and unwarlike. "I am getting to be an old man," he said. "I am at peace with everyone," he added. Then he, too, was gone.

Dr. Jared Daniels had worked thirty-six straight hours treating the wounded at Birch Coulie. He had neither eaten nor slept during that time. Armed with only his small surgical instrument kit, he had crawled from one wounded man to another and finally to the makeshift hospital tent, inspecting and binding wounds.

Despite what he had done for the soldiers at Birch Coulie, he remained a staunch advocate for the Dakota nation. He insisted that those who argued that the Sioux were a "wild and barbarous race" knew nothing about Indian character. The great cause of the Dakota War, he maintained, had been treaty obligations violated by the U.S. government. In 1869 Daniels was appointed by President Grant as Indian agent for the Sisseton Indians at Fort Wadsworth, South Dakota. There, he established schools, encouraged self-reliance, and healed the Indian sick. His influence, the Indians said, "was greater among Indians than any other white man." Indian chiefs praised him as honest and a "very good man." Eventually Dr. Daniels was appointed to oversee all Indian agencies in the West, and he traveled from Minnesota to Montana to Arizona, ensuring that his constructive ideas were carried out.

Although he died in 1904 in Pomona, California, his remains were returned for burial in the Minnesota River Valley, among the plum trees and beneath the river bluffs he loved.

"No man on any battlefield ever displayed more heroism," his obituary said. And no man knew that more than Robert K. Boyd, whose life Daniels had saved.

After the Battle of Birch Coulie, Lieutenant Timothy Sheehan also went off to the Civil War with Minnesota's Sixth Regiment. He was one of General Sherman's officers at Vicksburg.

Sheehan was wounded seven times during his Civil War service. At the Battle of Nashville six color bearers for the regiment were shot down during a charge on Rebel defenses. Finally, it was Sheehan who picked up the colors, received a mangling bayonet wound in his right hand, and led the advance across an open field. He was discharged as a lieutenant colonel and returned to Albert Lea, Minnesota, where he married and raised three sons.

Still eager to serve his adopted country however he could, in 1871 he ran for and was elected sheriff of Freeborn County. "Colonel," everyone called him as he went about his civic duties. A decade later he was appointed deputy U.S. marshal for Minnesota, and in the following year he submitted an application to President McKinley for the honor of serving as U.S. marshal for Minnesota. Those who supported his application wrote that he was the "personification of bravery." Sheehan had been "faithful as a dog" to his friends. He had been a "Minute Man at the gates of liberty."

His application was turned down. The young, vigorous lieutenant who had saved Fort Ridgely, made a perilous ride to bring reinforcements for Birch Coulie, and then been wounded seven times in the Civil War was too old and unfit to be a U.S. marshal the government said.

As if to prove them wrong, the "Colonel" led a squad of twenty fellow marshals against warring Chippewa Indians near Bear Island in Minnesota. Before the fight Sheehan walked among his men and implored them to "keep cool." The Chippewas were driven off, but a dozen of Sheehan's detachment were killed or wounded. He himself was shot three times—in the arm, across his stomach, and in his good left hand.

In December 1907 he was living in St. Paul. In old age he had the same long, handsome face and trim body of his younger days, but his hair had turned pigeon gray. And his pension of $18.50 a month was hardly enough for food. Despite the habit of self-reliance that had helped him make his way as an Irish immigrant in America, he had no choice but to submit an application for an increase in his pension. He was sick and infirm, he wrote, and no longer able to earn a livelihood. He suffered chronic diarrhea, and he had constant pain at various wound sites. He couldn't dress himself or even button his collar. He had become old and infirm, but after he died in St. Paul in 1912, he was eulogized as "a hero of the first order."

Little Crow, Big Eagle, Gray Bird, Red Iron, Little Paul, Captain Marsh, Dr. Daniels, General Sibley, Joseph Coursolle, Timothy Sheehan, they were all dead now. They had been chiefs and forceful speakers and head soldiers and doctors and prominent frontier scouts and captains and colonels and generals. They had all been much more noteworthy figures in the Battle of Birch Coulie than Robert K. Boyd, a young runaway who had swum raging rivers and climbed sheer cliffs in search of something more exciting than the day-to-day drudgery and boredom of his life in a frontier settlement. At the Battle of Birch Coulie he had been just a lowly enlisted man who hardly knew how to fire his musket. And despite his vow to "fight to the limit of my strength and endurance," he had done nothing heroic in the battle. In fact he had hardly gotten out of his tent before he had been struck down. Yet Boyd was the one standing now on the wood dais on Labor Day 1930, preparing to speak to a sea of thousands of faces assembled across a freshly plowed field of what had once been a bloody battleground.

In the years since the battle there had been intervening wars and grim battlegrounds such as Gettysburg, Little Big Horn, Wounded Knee, San Juan Hill, and Verdun. They had all been bloodier and costlier than the Battle of Birch Coulie, but as far as Boyd was concerned, none of those battlegrounds were any more hallowed or historic than the ground he now looked across.

The introduction for Boyd was brief. He was the last survivor of the Battle of Birch Coulie, and he was eighty-five years old. His eyes had turned milky and distant with age. As he walked in a shuffle to the cornstalk microphone, his head jutted forward and down as if he were gawking at something on the ground.

Over the years Boyd had given dozens of speeches to veterans groups, schoolchildren, church gatherings, and civic groups. He had also written about the battle again and again. He knew that as a writer and speaker he lacked "style" and "finish." But when he reached the microphone on the dais at Birch Coulie, the strength and clarity of voice was surprising, and he began to recite fluently from his memory exactly what he wanted to say.

"I came to tell you," he began, "of events that took place here a long time ago." It was a story, he said, that was "older than history and always the same, when a poor, ignorant, defrauded, and downtrodden people rise up in their wrath."

He paused, to let the importance of his opening sink in. Then he went on. "There are some who might expect me to describe the outrages committed by the most desperate and depraved of these Indians. But I shall not do so. We would not judge our own race by the acts of the criminals who are all too plenty in our own country."

No, the story he had to tell wasn't the traditional one of heroic cowboys defeating savage Indians. His story was different. It was the story of what had hung in the balance at Birch Coulie, with its brutal collision of two worlds and cultures. Would the frontier, and Minnesota in particular, continue to offer settlers the beguiling dream of cheap fertile land around peaceful prairie communities? Or would it become a battleground for the Dakotas' equally beguiling dream of the return of their ancestral lands?

For decades after the battle, Boyd knew, western Minnesota had remained a largely abandoned region. Those frontier settlers who had dreamed of fertile land and abundant crops had fled. The few Dakotas who slowly came back to the land of their ancestors "walked in single file over old trails, silent and aloof."

To help the audience appreciate what had been at stake, Boyd asked them to "put out of your minds all knowledge of the progress which the world has made during the last seventy years." He wanted them to forget cars, telephones, electric lights, and the flying machines out of which daring men had just parachuted and then drifted like white cottonwood seeds onto the battle site. Such images would only obscure the simple and stark reality of the collision of beguiling dreams at Birch Coulie.

"I want you to feel as if you are living in those early times," he said.

He went on to describe briefly how he had been tardy for a troop muster on the Fort Ridgely parade grounds and thus wound up assigned to the burial expedition as punishment. He described his painful wounds and where he had been on the battlefield when he received each one. He explained how Dr. Daniels had probed his shoulder wound with a "pliers" to remove bone fragments. But, he said, he had "always tried to ignore pain and discomfort, and this faculty has helped me through many hard places."

Then Boyd turned to the legacies of the battle. One of those legacies, he insisted, was that the War Department had revised its old battle tactics. White soldiers, he explained, had typically "stood up in the ranks and shot at an enemy also in ranks." The result was usually slaughter, as it had been in the Civil War. It was *not* true, he went on, that Indians fought like crazed, disorganized savages who hurled themselves with suicidal frenzy into pitched battle. Indians fought with ingenuity and organization, he insisted, and it had been the Dakotas who introduced the U.S. military to "skirmish fighting" as a replacement for foolish American battle tactics that were truly suicidal. It was, he said, a tactic that would be "with us until there becomes a radical change in modern warfare."

Boyd reminded the huge crowd that it had been nearly seventy years since the battle and the subsequent characterizations of the Dakotas as savages. But eventually prominent voices in Minnesota and elsewhere had begun to argue that "the world should know why Indians became numerous and great and strong before the lines of civilization fell upon them."

"The Indian," he went on, "while at peace and in his daily life is quiet in his ways, he never speaks a harsh word even while he is holding a feeling of resentment. For this reason there are many who have dealt with him over the years without knowing there is another side to his character."

One of those secret sides of Indian character, Boyd continued, was that they "had known from the very first that the whole reservation system was tainted with fraud." It was a foul system that left Indians with a smoldering resentment.

He turned to the subject of a proper memorial for the battleground. For more than thirty years after the battle, Boyd said, Birch Coulie had remained unmarked, unhonored. Then in 1894, after a committee had been formed to create a proper battlefield memorial, a fifty-two-foot-high granite obelisk had been mounted on the prairie, but *in the wrong place*, a mile from the battleground. Efforts to move the obelisk to the right spot had failed. Now thirty more years had passed, and Boyd wanted the grounds turned into a state park. To that end he had drawn elaborate maps of the battlefield, showing where the troops had been inside the horseshoe of wagons. Over the years local farmers had tilled and plowed the soil again and again until the battleground was now just a dirt field. Even the knoll behind which Big Eagle had concealed his men was gone. The battlefield should be "seeded to grass," Boyd said, "and brought as near as possible to its original state as wild prairie ground."

Finally, he apologized for remarks that might have seemed "disconnected and not in their right order." But he hoped that what he had said would give the listeners a better understanding of the Battle of Birch Coulie.

"In conclusion," he said, "I think the people of western Minnesota should preserve all places of historic interest, and use their best talent in making a true and complete record of all events" that had occurred at Birch Coulie. His point was that no one would ever be able to understand the upheavals of the present age — Depressions and Great Wars and Machine Age racket — without understanding the turbulence of the past.

He paused one last time to let that admonition sink in. Then he lifted his head and gazed over the sea of faces. In his youth, he admitted, he had been "vain and peculiar." He did not explain how "peculiar" he must have seemed when he asked his playground friends to stick pins in him. Nor did he explain how it was just that peculiar exercise that had helped him to survive at Birch Coulie.

"I wanted others to think that nothing could shock me," he went on, "that I had no nerves, no emotions, and that I never cried." It was as close as the sturdy survivor could come to admitting that his recollections of the battle in old age were filled with emotions and regret.

"But all this," he said and lifted one arm to sweep the landscape, "is in the past." The white man had taken for his own what had been in that past the "wild country, the land of the buffalo, the elk, and the antelope." It was a past of a simpler, half-wild life, and it was gone, it was gone. None of them, Boyd said, could ever go back to it.

Boyd thanked the audience for listening, then shuffled away from the microphone exactly as he had approached it, head down and eyes lowered. In the brief silence before the applause broke out, the audience could hear the distant drone of a tractor, grinding its claws into tableland that Boyd wanted preserved and seeded to grass.

The next day Boyd returned to his home in Eau Claire, Wisconsin, where he had been living for forty years. Two years later Robert K. Boyd, the last survivor of the Battle of Birch Coulie, was also dead.

In 1978 plans were laid by the Minnesota Historical Society for a Birch Coulie battlefield site. But it was twenty years before the plans were completed, with a convenient walking path and guideposts marking the site where the horseshoe of wagons had formed and the knoll behind which Big Eagle and his men had hidden. The prairie grasses were allowed to grow again, restoring the deep cover through which the first attackers had crawled.

Despite the effort to keep the memory of the Battle of Birch Coulie alive, that effort was often lost in present and future concerns. Farm neighbors, for instance, complained of foul odors because of modern pollution of the Birch Coulie stream. Then in 2000 a news story pictured children on a school picnic sliding down a mudslide improvised on the steep banks of the coulie. What recollections there were of the history of the battle site and its importance to the two cultures who had had so much at stake seemed lost.

Finally, some scientists predicted the inevitable coming of another Ice Age, with the same kind of glacial bulldozer that carved the coulie ten thousand years earlier. Their predictions were that the silent remains of Birch Coulie and the spirit of the Dakota and white soldiers who fought there would eventually lie buried and forgotten beneath a patchwork of prairie sloughs.

Acknowledgments

An army of researchers, writers, historians, and friends provided information and encouragement. Among them were Tom Ellig, Duane Bright, Alan Woolworth, Jerry Anderson, Dave Craigmile, Scott Larson, Dan Fjeld, Rhoda Gilman, Bob Sandeen, Ron Manzow, Marcia Anderson, Dr. Roger Christgau, Tom Schleck, Jon Brings Three White Horses, and Frank Bettendorf.

Numerous archives and institutions were critical sources of information: National Archives and Records Administration, Redwood County Historical Society, Nicollet County Historical Society, Minnesota Historical Society, Oyate Research Center, Plainview History Association, Fort Ridgely Interpretive Center, Freeborn County Historical Society, and San Mateo County Interlibrary Loan Desk.

Finally, I am particularly grateful to Jill Wohnoutka, who on my behalf combed the Renville County Historical Society's extensive archives for documents on the Birch Coulie battle.

Sources

The source citations are arranged by page number and identify the sources for subject and topic areas as they appear in a paragraph or pages of text. For repeated book and newspaper citations, the initial reference contains a complete title or story headline. Subsequent references to the same source repeat only an abbreviated title or headline.

Preface

vii **The Battle of Birch Coulie and the Dakota War of 1862:** Roy Meyer, *History of the Santee Sioux* (Lincoln: University of Nebraska Press, 1967), 294–316, 352, 357, 364–65; notes from a telephone interview with Dennis Neumann, United Tribes Technical College, September 15, 2009; Gerald S. Henig, "A Neglected Cause of the Sioux Uprising," *Minnesota History*, Fall 1976, 107–10; David E. Larsen, "Some Native Thoughts on the Quincentennial," *Minnesota History*, Spring 1992, 26–31; Willoughby Babcock, "Minnesota's Indian War," *Minnesota History*, September 1962, 93–98; Linda Grover, "Indian School," *Minnesota History*, Winter 2002–3, 2; Governor Rudy Perpich, "Minnesota History and Heritage," *Minnesota History*, Summer 1977, 245–49; Raymond Wilson, "Forty Years to Judgment," *Minnesota History*, Fall 1981, 285–91; "Jackpot Junction Casino Hotel, Morton MN," http://www.

jackpotjunction.com (accessed September 23, 2009); Robert K. Boyd, "Notes and Documents: The Birch Cooley Monument," *Minnesota History*, September 1931, 297–301; Michael Clodfelter, *The Dakota War: The United States Army versus the Sioux, 1862–1865* (Jefferson NC: McFarland, 1998), 221; Dennis Neumann, e-mail to author, September 25, 2009; Vine Deloria and Clifford Lytle, *The Nations Within: The Past and Future of American Indian Sovereignty* (Austin: University of Texas Press, 1998), 234–35; James Olson and Raymond Wilson, *Native Americans in the Twentieth Century* (Urbana: University of Illinois Press, 1986), 131–33; Nick Coleman, "Jerk the Strings," *Minnesota Monthly*, October 2001, http://www.mnstate.edu/mla/PortfolioFirstSample. pdf (accessed September 27, 2009).

1. Private Robert K. Boyd

1 **It was the morning of August 31:** J. J. Egan, "The Battle of Birch Coulie, September 2, 1862," undated, 3, Renville County Historical Society, Morton MN (hereafter RCHS); "Captain Grant's Account of a Reconnaissance Expedition," *Morton Enterprise*, February 12, 1892; Captain Joseph Anderson to Dr. J. W. Daniels, August 13, 1894, Minnesota Historical Society, St. Paul (hereafter MHS); Charles Fisk, "The First Fifty Years of Recorded Weather History in Minnesota, 1820–1869," http://home.att.net/~station_climo/purpose.htm (accessed August 2, 2008); Robert K. Boyd, "What a Boy Saw at Ft. Ridgely," Fort Ridgely State Park, Fairfax MN; *Minnesota in the Civil and Indian Wars, 1861–65* (St. Paul: Pioneer Press Company, 1890), 306, 731 (hereafter *MCIW*); Gary Anderson and Alan Woolworth, eds., *Through Dakota Eyes: Narrative Accounts of the Minnesota Indian War of 1862* (St. Paul: Minnesota Historical Society Press, 1988), 165; Kenneth Carley, *The Sioux Uprising of 1862* (St. Paul: Minnesota Historical Society, 1961), 48.

2 **Each man of the expedition:** *MCIW*, 731; B. H. Goodell, "Personal Recollections of the Sioux Massacre of 1862," April 10, 1895, 12, MHS.

2 **For drill at Fort Snelling:** *MCIW*, 304; Captain Richard Strout, "Biography," http://www.dxhansen.com/sshubbard2-0/p39 (accessed August 15, 2008); Francis Lord, *They Fought for the Union* (New York: Bonanza Books, 1960), 140–43, 154–55, 162.

2 **Some of the men felt:** Anderson to Daniels, August 13, 1894; "Member of Grant's Command Recalls Birch Coulie Fight," *Morton Enterprise*,

May 30, 1929; "The Battle of Birch Coulie as Taken from Memoirs," *Morton Enterprise*, August 24, 1939; Duane Schultz, *Over the Earth I Come: The Great Sioux Uprising of 1862* (New York: St. Martin's Press, 1993), 202; "Birch Coulie Monument," *Morton Enterprise*, May 18, 1894; Alonzo Emery, *A Thrilling Narrative of the Sioux War of 1862–3* (Chicago: Connally, 1896), 112–27; Anderson to Daniels, August 13, 1894; E. W. Earle, "Reminiscences of the Sioux Massacre in 1862," 23, MHS; Anderson and Woolworth, *Through Dakota Eyes*, 166; MCIW, 307; Bob Boyd, "The Indian War Outbreak," undated, 9–10, RCHS.

2 **Other soldiers felt:** "Birch Coulie Battle Called the Crux of the Indian Outbreak," *Morton Enterprise*, October 22, 1931; Wayne Webb and J. I. Swedberg, *Redwood: The Story of a County* (Redwood Falls MN: Redwood County Board of Commissioners, 1964), 48–51; G. G. Alanson, "Stirring Adventures of the J. R. Brown Family," *Sacred Heart News*, undated, 3, 15; Boyd, "Indian War Outbreak," 9; MCIW, 736; Thomas Hughes, *Indian Chiefs of Southern Minnesota* (Minneapolis: Ross and Haines, 1969), 22, 27, 80; Carley, *Sioux Uprising*, 49; Anderson to Daniels, August 13, 1894.

3 **No soldier worked harder:** Boyd, "Indian War Outbreak," 4, 5, 7, 8, 12; MCIW, 338; Robert Boyd, "The Battle of Birch Coulie: A Wounded Man's Description of a Battle with Indians," address given at Eau Claire WI, January 1925, 4–5, 8–9, RCHS; Boyd, "What a Boy Saw"; "Sixth Regiment," http://Rootsweb.ancestry.com (accessed August 24, 2008).

5 **At one point during the work:** Boyd, "Indian War Outbreak," 9; Boyd, "Battle of Birch Coulie: A Wounded Man's Description," 9.

5 **While the grave diggers:** Boyd, "Indian War Outbreak," 9–10; Boyd, "Battle of Birch Coulie: A Wounded Man's Description," 9.

6 **The soldier quickly tried:** "Member of Grant's Command."

6 **Brown argued for camping:** Earle, "Reminiscences," 1; Anderson to Daniels, August 13, 1894; Egan, "Battle of Birch Coulie," 2; Carley, *Sioux Uprising*, 49; Boyd, "Indian War Outbreak," 10–11; MCIW, 305; Henry H. Sibley to Minnesota adjutant general O. Malmros, "Report on the Battle of Birch Coulie," September 4, 1862, MHS; Rev. Moses Adams, "Sioux Outbreak in 1862," http://www.sleepyeye.org/Dakota2 (accessed August 5, 2008).

7 **The first suspicion:** Schultz, *Over the Earth*, 46, 189; Anderson and Woolworth, *Through Dakota Eyes*, 57, 159–60; Mary Bakeman, *Legends, Letters, Lies: Readings on Inkpaduta and the Spirit Lake Massacre* (Roseville MM: Park Genealogical Books, 2001), 21, 44, 48–49, 70, 82, 84, 120; Joe Coursolle, "The Spirit Lake Massacre," *Henderson Democrat*, May 7, 1857; "Joe Coursolle," http://forefolk.homestead.com (accessed August 25, 2008).

8 **As the expedition moved:** Anderson and Woolworth, *Through Dakota Eyes*, 161.

8 **Then he spotted:** Dr. Jared Daniels, "Indian Outbreak of 1862," 12, MHS.

9 **Of all the grisly burials:** MCIW, 306; Schultz, *Over the Earth*, 53–55, 189–90; C. M. Oehler, *The Great Sioux Outbreak* (New York: Da Capo Press, 1997), 150; "Fled from the Sioux," *Morton Enterprise*, September 15, 1911; Earle, "Reminiscences," 28; "Captain Grant's Account."

9 **As Corporal Joseph Coursolle dug:** Anderson and Woolworth, *Through Dakota Eyes*, 161.

10 **Her name was Justina Kreiger:** MCIW, 307.

11 **It was on the open prairie:** MCIW, 306–7; Daniels, "Indian Outbreak," 10; Charles E. Flandreau, *The Battle of Birch Coulie*, 159–60, gutenberg.org/ebooks/25677 (accessed August 13, 2008); "The Birth of the Birch Coulee," March 1992, RCHS; author's tour of the Birch Coulie battlefield, September 20–21, 2008; Frank Moore, "Reminiscences of Pioneer Days in St. Paul," http://fullbooks.com (accessed August 15, 2008); "He Fought at Birch Coulie," *Morton Enterprise*, June 25, 1909; Anderson to Daniels, August 13, 1894; Carley, *Sioux Uprising*, 48, 50; Daniels, "Indian Outbreak," 11; Joseph R. Brown, "Battle of Birch Coulie," M582—Dakota Conflict of 1862, Manuscript Collection, MHS; Sibley to Malmros, September 4, 1862; John Riehle, "Bloodshed at Birch Coulie," undated, RCHS.

12 **Then he directed his teamsters:** Boyd, "Battle of Birch Coulie: A Wounded Man's Description," 4, 10–11; "Battle of Birch Coulie Was the Crux of the Indian Outbreak," *Olivia Times*, September 1932.

12 **One of Major Brown's cavalry officers:** Anderson to Daniels, August 13, 1894; Oehler, *Great Sioux Outbreak*, 169; MCIW, 308.

12 **As Joe Coursolle laid:** Anderson and Woolworth, *Through Dakota Eyes*, 161–62.

13 **Finally, Major Brown walked:** *MCIW*, 35; Daniels, "Indian Outbreak," 13; Carley, *Sioux Uprising*, 50; Anderson and Woolworth, *Through Dakota Eyes*, 162.

2. Red Iron

14 **No one in the mid-nineteenth century** Webb and Swedberg, *Redwood*, 8, 11; B. J. Lossing, *Pictorial Field Book of the Revolution*, vol. 2 (New York: Harper, 1860), 205, 449; George Catlin, *North American Indians*, vol. 2 (Minneapolis: Ross and Haines, 1965), 145, 161, 172, 238.

15 **These observers described:** Catlin, *North American Indians*, 190–91, 193, 195, 232–35, 242; Frank Mayer, *With Pen and Pencil on the Frontier in 1851* (St. Paul: Minnesota Historical Society, 1932), 190–91, 193, 195; William Folwell, *The History of Minnesota*, vol. 1 (St. Paul: Minnesota Historical Society, 1922), 170; Mari Sandoz, *Love Song to the Plains* (Lincoln: University of Nebraska Press, 1961), 175–76, 180–86.

15 **The first white pioneers in the new land:** Lossing, *Pictorial Field Book*, 46, 288; Mayer, *With Pen and Pencil*, 99, 139, 152, 157; *Collections of the Minnesota Historical Society*, vol. 9 (St. Paul: Minnesota Historical Society, 1901), 417; Folwell, *History of Minnesota*, 183, 272; Catlin, *North American Indians*, 166, 241; Daniel Buck, *Indian Outbreaks* (Minneapolis: Ross and Haines, 1965), 15, 77; Webb and Swedberg, *Redwood*, 14; Roxanne Dunbar Ortiz, *The Great Sioux Nation: Sitting in Judgment on America* (n.p.: Moon Books, 1977), 56, 121; Folwell, *History of Minnesota*, 150.

16 **The first settlers who came:** Webb and Swedberg, *Redwood*, 18; Lossing, *Pictorial Field Book*, 45–46, 288; Buck, *Indian Outbreaks*, 14; Jonathan Raban, *Bad Land: An American Romance* (New York: Vintage Departure, 1960), 40; Ortiz, *Great Sioux Nation*, 84.

16 **In an effort to lure:** Mayer, *With Pen and Pencil*, vii; Webb and Swedberg, *Redwood*, 5; William Sherman, ed., *Plains Folk: North Dakota's Ethnic History* (Fargo: North Dakota Institute for Regional Studies, 1988), 3; *Collections of the Minnesota Historical Society*, vol. 9, 281, 589; Folwell, *History of Minnesota*, 159, 351; Ortiz, *Great Sioux Nation*, 20; Catlin, *North American Indians*, 201; *Minnesota: The Empire State* (n.p.: Board of Immigration for the State of Minnesota, 1878), 65.

17 **The missionaries came:** Folwell, *History of Minnesota*, 170; Mayer, *With Pen and Pencil*, 130, 132; Ortiz, *Great Sioux Nation*, 19, 134; Buck, *Indian Outbreaks*, 77; *Collections of the Minnesota Historical Society*, vol. 9, 280; Webb and Swedberg, *Redwood*, 50.

17 **Along with the missionaries:** Webb and Swedberg, *Redwood*, 31; Catlin, *North American Indians*, 162; Lossing, *Pictorial Field Book*, 204–5.

18 **However, the government went:** Hughes, *Indian Chiefs*, 23; "Nicollet County," http://mnhs.org/places (accessed August 8, 2008); Rhoda Gilman, *Henry Hastings Sibley: Divided Heart* (St. Paul: Minnesota Historical Society, 2004), 124, 126; Webb and Swedberg, *Redwood*, 38–39; Folwell, *History of Minnesota*, 272; Hughes, *Indian Chiefs*, 23; Carley, *Sioux Uprising*, 11–12; Schultz, *Over the Earth*, 58–60; *Collections of the Minnesota Historical Society*, vol. 9, 127–28; Gary Anderson, *Little Crow: Spokesman for the Sioux* (St. Paul: Minnesota Historical Society, 1986), 9; Isaac Heard, *History of the Sioux War and Massacre of 1862–1863*, http://google.com.books/PDF/history-of-the-Sioux-war (accessed October 11–12, 2008); Buck, *Indian Outbreaks*, 60, 62, 75; Webb and Swedberg, *Redwood*, 37–38; Theodore Blegen, *Minnesota: A History of the State* (Minneapolis: University of Minnesota Press, 1975), 66–69, 174; Meyer, *History of the Santee Sioux*, 81–83.

20 **Chief Red Iron was leader:** Hughes, *Indian Chiefs*, 98; Heard, *History of the Sioux War*, 36–37, 41, 85, 94–95; Buck, *Indian Outbreaks*, 69.

21 **Land fever erupted:** Folwell, *History of Minnesota*, 354–55, 359–63; Buck, *Indian Outbreaks*, 10; Mari Sandoz, *Crazy Horse: The Strange Man of the Oglalas* (Hastings: Knopf, 1942), 128–29; Buck, *Indian Outbreaks*, 59; Webb and Swedberg, *Redwood*, 68; Sherman, *Plains Folk*, 14, 64.

21 **Life along that frontier:** Catlin, *North American Indians*, 223–24, 242–45, 250, 256; Webb and Swedberg, *Redwood*, 41; *Collections of the Minnesota Historical Society*, vol. 9, 240.

21 **On their new reservations:** Buck, *Indian Outbreaks*, 62, 75; Heard, *History of the Sioux War*, 18, 21, 27, 31, 33, 50; Hughes, *Indian Chiefs*, 99; Gilman, *Henry Hastings Sibley*, 70, 124, 170; Schultz, *Over the Earth*, 23; Anderson and Woolworth, *Through Dakota Eyes*, 12, 23; Carley, *Sioux Uprising*, 12; Schultz, *Over the Earth*, 9; Mayer, *With Pen and Pencil*, 145; Folwell, *History of Minnesota*, 354; Buck, *Indian Outbreaks*, 27–30, 60, 77–79; Carley, *Sioux Uprising*, 13; Ortiz, *Great Sioux Nation*, 22; Ignatius Donnelly, "History of the Indian War," August 29, 1862, 212, MHS.

23 **Back on the two reservations:** Sherman, *Plains Folk*, 14; Henry David Thoreau, *The Writings of Henry David Thoreau*, 448, http:// google.com/books?id (accessed September 7, 2008); tape-recorded interview with Tom Ellig, Morton MN, September 19, 2008; Carley, *Sioux Uprising*, 14; Anderson and Woolworth, *Through Dakota Eyes*, 20; Webb and Swedberg, *Redwood*, 59; Anderson, *Little Crow*, 116; "Minnesota Weather, 1862," http://home.att.net/-station_climo/yr1562 (accessed August 21, 2008); Brown, "Battle of Birch Coulie"; Earle, "Reminiscences," 3.

23 **Five thousand Dakotas:** Heard, *History of the Sioux War*, 18, 47; Timothy Sheehan, "Report of Notes Kept by Timothy Sheehan," June 18–November 6, 1862, Fort Ridgely State Park, Fairfax MN; Schultz, *Over the Earth*, 11; Webb and Swedberg, *Redwood*, 62–63; Daniels, "Indian Outbreak," 23; *MCIW*, 247.

23 **Despite the presence of the soldiers:** Sheehan, "Report of Notes"; *MCIW*, 245.

24 **At the Lower Agency:** Heard, *History of the Sioux War*, 48; Anderson, *Little Crow*, 127–28; Carley, *Sioux Uprising*, 15; Anderson and Woolworth, *Through Dakota Eyes*, 24, 32, 38; Hughes, *Indian Chiefs*, 68.

24 **This statement lit the fuse:** Hughes, *Indian Chiefs*, 29; Heard, *History of the Sioux War*, 52; Carley, *Sioux Uprising*, 16–17; Anderson and Woolworth, *Through Dakota Eyes*, 35, 38.

25 **A council of one hundred men:** Anderson and Woolworth, *Through Dakota Eyes*, 13, 27, 29–30, 34, 53; Schultz, *Over the Earth*, 33; Anderson, *Little Crow*, 130–31; Earle, "Reminiscences," 4, 36; Hughes, *Indian Chiefs*, 23, 31, 68; Carley, *Sioux Uprising*, 18–19.

3. Little Crow

27 **His name was Little Crow:** Hughes, *Indian Chiefs*, 23, 50, 52–58; Anderson, *Little Crow*, 9, 35, 37–40, 44, 48, 63, 70, 75, 103, 142; Schultz, *Over the Earth*, 34–35; Anderson and Woolworth, *Through Dakota Eyes*, 39; Webb and Swedberg, *Redwood*, 33; Earle, "Reminiscences," 4, 37; Daniels, "Indian Outbreak," 22–23; "Sketches Historical and Descriptions of the Monuments and Tablets Erected by the Minnesota State Historical Society in Renville and Redwood Counties," Minnesota Valley Historical Society, http://rrcnet.org.org/-historical/monument (accessed August 5, 2008); Gilman, *Henry Hastings Sibley*, 97; Oehler, *Great Sioux Outbreak*, 20; Carley, *Sioux Uprising*, 70.

29 **Little Crow was fifty-two:** Anderson, *Little Crow*, 108, 121, 131, 167; Brown, "Battle of Birch Coulie"; Heard, *History of the Sioux War,* 59–60; Anderson and Woolworth, *Through Dakota Eyes*, 4, 6, 12–13, 20, 27, 34, 36, 39–40, 54, 149; Carley, *Sioux Uprising*, 19; Gilman, *Henry Hastings Sibley*, 171; Oehler, *Great Sioux Outbreak*, 21; "Sketches Historical"; Webb and Swedberg, *Redwood*, 53; Hughes, *Indian Chiefs*, 56.

30 **His name was Big Eagle:** Webb and Swedberg, *Redwood*, 52; Hughes, *Indian Chiefs*, 59–62; Anderson and Woolworth, *Through Dakota Eyes*, 21, 26, 55–56, 147; "Sketches Historical"; Oehler, *Great Sioux Outbreak*, 158; Anderson, *Little Crow*, 22, 141, 149.

31 **Red Middle Voice, chief:** Anderson and Woolworth, *Through Dakota Eyes*, 26, 40; Schultz, *Over the Earth*, 41; Heard, *History of the Sioux War,* 59–60; Hughes, *Indian Chiefs*, 30–31.

31 **Little Crow came to his feet:** Schultz, *Over the Earth*, 8, 15, 40–41; Anderson and Woolworth, *Through Dakota Eyes*, 25–26, 62, 69; Heard, *History of the Sioux War,* 46; Earle, "Reminiscences," 36; Gilman, *Henry Hastings Sibley*, 177; Brown, "Battle of Birch Coulie"; Hughes, *Indian Chiefs*, 54–55; Carley, *Sioux Uprising*, 19; Anderson, *Little Crow*, 132.

33 **Once the Dakotas were armed:** Anderson and Woolworth, *Through Dakota Eyes*, 13, 56, 62–63, 82, 103–4, 129, 144; Earle, "Reminiscences," 4; Gilman, *Henry Hastings Sibley*, 181; Brown, "Battle of Birch Coulie"; Heard, *History of the Sioux War,* 134–37; Webb and Swedberg, *Redwood*, 76; Heard, *History of the Sioux War,* 62, 68; Carley, *Sioux Uprising*, 19, 28, 31, 52–53; MCIW, 302.

33 **The worst incident:** MCIW, 307; Schultz, *Over the Earth*, 53–55, 189–90; Oehler, *Great Sioux Outbreak*, 150; "Fled from the Sioux"; "Captain Grant's Account."

34 **The first encouraging victory:** MCIW, 305, 731; Daniels, "Indian Outbreak," 12; Carley, *Sioux Uprising*, 22–24; Anderson, *Little Crow*, 38; Lucius Hubbard and R. I. Holcombe, *Minnesota in Three Centuries,* vol. 3 (Mankato MN: Mankato Free Press, 1908), 314.

34 **On the Upper Agency:** Anderson and Woolworth, *Through Dakota Eyes*, 99, 120–23.

34 **Dakota soldiers from the Upper Agency:** Anderson, *Little Crow*, 140; Schultz, *Over the Earth*, 101.

35 **The first question for Little Crow:** "Sketches Historical"; Brown,

"Battle of Birch Coulie"; MCIW, 260; Anderson and Woolworth, *Through Dakota Eyes*, 24, 131, 146, 154, 268; Heard, *History of the Sioux War*, 61.

35 **Some of the chiefs:** Anderson, *Little Crow*, 143; Schultz, *Over the Earth*, 72, 94, 96; MCIW, 731; Anderson and Woolworth, *Through Dakota Eyes*, 146.

36 **Despite the scouts' report:** Carley, *Sioux Uprising*, 38, 42–43; Schultz, *Over the Earth*, 99, 101–2; Anderson and Woolworth, *Through Dakota Eyes*, 147, 157, 172; Heard, *History of the Sioux War*, 78–80.

36 **Meanwhile, that night at Fort Ridgely:** Anderson and Woolworth, *Through Dakota Eyes*, 59, 94–95, 137–38, 148–49, 154–57, 159–60, 172; Carley, *Sioux Uprising*, 32–34, 35, 37; Earle, "Reminiscences," 19–22; Schultz, *Over the Earth*, 46, 102, 115–18, 120, 145, 149; Goodell, "Personal Recollections," 15, 21, 27, 31, 35, 37, 39–40; Sheehan, "Report of Notes"; Heard, *History of the Sioux War*, 83–84; Anderson, *Little Crow*, 143–45; Boyd, "Indian War Outbreak"; MCIW, 731; Heard, *History of the Sioux War*, 83–84; MCIW, 310; Hubbard and Holcombe, *Minnesota in Three Centuries*, 337–39; "Minnesota Weather, 1862"; "Sketches Historical"; Oehler, *Great Sioux Outbreak*, 124.

4. Gray Bird

39 **A lone rider:** Boyd, "Battle of Birch Coulie: A Wounded Man's Description"; Daniels, "Indian Outbreak," 7; Anderson and Woolworth, *Through Dakota Eyes*, 14; Schultz, *Over the Earth*, 257–58; Moore, "Reminiscences."

40 **Ramsey had quickly picked:** MCIW, 147, 302, 350, 712, 735; Anderson and Woolworth, *Through Dakota Eyes*, 67; Oehler, *Great Sioux Outbreak*, 136; Gilman, *Henry Hastings Sibley*, 12, 20, 24, 32, 108, 153, 156, 168, 174, 177, 180; Webb and Swedberg, *Redwood*, 30; Heard, *History of the Sioux War*, 118; Carley, *Sioux Uprising*, 47; Goodell, "Personal Recollections," 12–13; Boyd, "Battle of Birch Coulie: A Wounded Man's Description"; "Battle of Birch Coulie Memorial," *Morton Enterprise*, March 31, 1893; "The Battle of Birch Coulie," *Morton Enterprise*, July 29, 1926.

40 **On the day that Little Crow:** interview with Duane Bright, San Mateo CA, July 22, 2008; "Belgian Muskets," http://geocities.com/pentagon/barracks/3627 (accessed July 10, 2008); "Springfield Model 1861," http://en.wikipedia.org/wiki/Springfield; "Chronicles of the

American Civil War," http://pddoc.com/cw-chronicles (accessed July 10, 2008); Cyril Upham, "Arms and Equipment for the Iowa Troops in the Civil War," *Iowa Journal of History and Politics*, January 1918; Boyd, "What a Boy Saw"; MCIW, 158, 255, 302, 304, 350, 698, 734; Carley, *Sioux Uprising*, 37; Anderson, *Little Crow*, 153; Boyd, "Battle of Birch Coulie: A Wounded Man's Description"; Sibley to Malmros, September 4, 1862; Lord, *They Fought for the Union*, 154–55.

41 **Little Crow and two dozen:** Anderson and Woolworth, *Through Dakota Eyes*, 145, 168–69; Anderson, *Little Crow*, 146; Schultz, *Over the Earth*, 180–81.

43 **With so much disagreement:** Anderson and Woolworth, *Through Dakota Eyes*, 162, 168–71, 194, 198–99, 201–2; Schultz, *Over the Earth*, 180, 183–84, 186–87; Anderson, *Little Crow*, 146, 153.

43 **The speaker for the Upper Agency:** Schultz, *Over the Earth*, 180, 183–85; Anderson and Woolworth, *Through Dakota Eyes*, 168, 194–95, 198; Anderson, *Little Crow*, 152–53, 188.

44 **Sitting in the circle:** Anderson, *Little Crow*, 153–55; Schultz, *Over the Earth*, 191; Anderson and Woolworth, *Through Dakota Eyes*, 168–69; Heard, *History of the Sioux War*, 134–37; MCIW, 304–5, 730, 737; Hughes, *Indian Chiefs*, 91; Daniels, "Indian Outbreak," 24; "Sketches Historical"; Egan, "Battle of Birch Coulie," 6; Harriet Bishop McConkey, *Dakota War Whoop* (Minneapolis: Ross and Haines, 1970), 179–80; "Bloodshed at Birch Coulie."

45 **Half of Little Crow's men:** Anderson and Woolworth, *Through Dakota Eyes*, 144; Franklin Wedge, *The History of Renville County Minnesota*, vol. 1 (Chicago: Cooper, 1916), 165.

46 **But from the vantage point:** Anderson, *Little Crow*, 153–55; Carley, *Sioux Uprising*, 49–50, 52; Anderson and Woolworth, *Through Dakota Eyes*, 91, 150; Oehler, *Great Sioux Outbreak*, 163–64, 168, 170; Schultz, *Over the Earth*, 191–92; Egan, "Battle of Birch Coulie," 6; MCIW, 304–5, 730; Heard, *History of the Sioux War*, 134–37; "Sketches Historical"; *Collections of the Minnesota Historical Society*, vol. 9, 394; "Bloodshed at Birch Coulie"; Hubbard and Holcombe, *Minnesota in Three Centuries*, 347; Wedge, *History of Renville County*, 165.

47 **Gray Bird, with three other Dakota chiefs:** Hughes, *Indian Chiefs*, 54, 59, 71–71; "Sketches Historical"; Schultz, *Over the Earth*, 193;

Anderson and Woolworth, *Through Dakota Eyes*, 144, 150; Wedge, *History of Renville County*, 166; "How the Indians Fought," *Morton Enterprise*, August 5, 1926; "Sketches Historical"; Carley, *Sioux Uprising*, 50.

5. Gaboo

48 **Just before dawn:** MCIW, 737; Carley, *Sioux Uprising*, 50; "Sketches Historical"; Anderson to Daniels, August 13, 1894; Wedge, *History of Renville County*, 166.

48 **As the cook crawled:** Egan, "Battle of Birch Coulie," 5; Carley, *Sioux Uprising*, 50–51; "Sketches Historical"; MCIW, 305, 308; Anderson and Woolworth, *Through Dakota Eyes*, 150; "Survivor Tells of Indian Warfare," *Morton Enterprise*, October 9, 1930.

49 **Suddenly, a brightly painted Indian:** Egan, "Battle of Birch Coulie," 1–6.

50 **Grant was the first:** Earle, "Reminiscences," 29–30, 32; Daniels, "Indian Outbreak," 13; MCIW, 305, 308; Emery, *Thrilling Narrative*, 113; Boyd, "Battle of Birch Coulie: A Wounded Man's Description"; Carley, *Sioux Uprising*, 51; Anderson and Woolworth, *Through Dakota Eyes*, 150, 162; "Captain Grant's Account"; "Sketches Historical"; "How the Indians Fought"; Anderson to Daniels, August 13, 1894; "Birch Coulie as Taken from Memoirs"; Joseph Anderson to Major Brown, September 4, 1862, MHS; Anderson to Daniels, August 13, 1894; "Descriptions of the Battle of Birch Coulie: Report of Hiram P. Grant," *Morton Enterprise*, August 23, 1912; Schultz, *Over the Earth*, 194; Egan, "Battle of Birch Coulie," 3; MCIW, 736.

50 **Meanwhile, most of the ninety-six horses:** Alanson, "Stirring Adventures," 15; Carley, *Sioux Uprising*, 51; MCIW, 308, 737–38; "Bloodshed at Birch Coulie"; Egan, "Battle of Birch Coulie," 5; "Captain Grant's Account."

50 **The first shots woke:** Boyd, "Indian War Outbreak," 11–12; Brown, "Battle of Birch Coulie"; Boyd, "Battle of Birch Coulie: A Continuance of the Story," *Morton Enterprise*, September 2, 1926; Boyd, "Battle of Birch Coulie: A Wounded Man's Description," 11; "Survivor Tells of Indian Warfare"; Robert Boyd, "Battle of Birch Coulie: Review and Outline of the Conditions," *Morton Enterprise*, August 19, 1926.

52 **Still, there were pockets:** "Birch Coulie as Taken from Memoirs"; Anderson to Daniels, August 13, 1894; Eagan, "Battle of Birch Coulie,"5; MCIW, 737–38; Anderson and Woolworth, *Through Dakota Eyes*, 151–52; Anderson to Brown, September 4, 1862.

53 **Major Brown continued to walk:** Carley, *Sioux Uprising*, 51; Egan, "Battle of Birch Coulie," 3; Hubbard and Holcombe, *Minnesota in Three Centuries*, 349; Alanson, "Stirring Adventures," 16; Emery, *Thrilling Narrative*, 116; Brown, "Battle of Birch Coulie."

53 **In one of the rifle pits:** battlefield markers, State Historic Site: Birch Coulie Battlefield, Morton MN; Carley, *Sioux Uprising*, 51; Egan, "Battle of Birch Coulie," 6, 114–15, 126; "How the Indians Fought"; Earle, "Reminiscences," 33; MCIW, 308, 737; Daniels, "Indian Outbreak," 14; Heard, *History of the Sioux War*, 135; Anderson to Daniels, August 13, 1894.

53 **In one of the wagons:** Oehler, *Great Sioux Outbreak*, 172; Carley, *Sioux Uprising*, 51; Boyd, "What a Boy Saw."

54 **One of the surviving horses:** "Bloodshed at Birch Coulie"; "Captain Grant's Account"; MCIW, 308, 737; Egan, "Battle of Birch Coulie," 5.

54 **From his firing position:** Anderson and Woolworth, *Through Dakota Eyes*, 57, 163; *Collections of the Minnesota Historical Society*, vol. 9, 276; Bakeman, *Legends, Letters, Lies*, 44, 70, 73, 75, 82, 84–85, 125.

56 **Corporal Joseph Coursolle was one:** MCIW, 308, 737; Anderson and Woolworth, *Through Dakota Eyes*, 163.

57 **It was then that one of the soldiers:** Anderson and Woolworth, *Through Dakota Eyes*, 163; MCIW, 306; Emery, *Thrilling Narrative*, 114.

58 **Some of the men took powder:** Anderson and Woolworth, *Through Dakota Eyes*, 163; Emery, *Thrilling Narrative*, 114.

58 **But a midmorning sun:** "Veteran Writes New Version of Battle of Birch Coulie," *Morton Enterprise*, November 7, 1913; MCIW, 308–9; "Birch Coulie as Taken from Memoirs."

58 **Inside the hospital tent:** Boyd, "Indian War Outbreak," 11; Brown, "Battle of Birch Coulie"; Boyd, "Battle of Birch Coulie: A Continuance."

59 **Then the deep boom:** MCIW, 738; Egan, "Battle of Birch Coulie," 5.

6. Colonel Sam McPhail and Lieutenant Sheehan

60 **One of those Fort Ridgely pickets:** Egan, "Battle of Birch Coulie," 6; Daniels, "Indian Outbreak," 17; "Greetings from Sleepy Eye

Minnesota," http://sleepyeye.org; "Bloodshed at Birch Coulie"; *MCIW*, 306, 338; "Veteran Writes New Version"; Boyd, "What a Boy Saw"; Heard, *History of the Sioux War*, 132.

61 **He ordered one:** Webb and Swedberg, *Redwood*, 119–20; Anderson and Woolworth, *Through Dakota Eyes*, 168.

61 **Many of the men were still recuperating:** Brown, "Battle of Birch Coulie"; "Greetings"; "Bloodshed at Birch Coulie"; *MCIW*, 167; Wedge, *History of Renville County*, 167; Carley, *Sioux Uprising*, 51; Goodell, "Personal Recollections," 49; Hubbard and Holcombe, *Minnesota in Three Centuries*, 349; "Sketches Historical."

62 **Meanwhile, uncertain of the terrain:** "Bloodshed at Birch Coulie"; "Sketches Historical"; "Veteran Writes New Version"; Brown, "Battle of Birch Coulie"; Daniels, "Indian Outbreak," 17.

62 **McPhail sent two scouts:** "Sketches Historical"; Emery, *Thrilling Narrative*, 121; Schultz, *Over the Earth*, 197–98; Anderson and Woolworth, *Through Dakota Eyes*, 152; *MCIW*, 308–9.

63 **McPhail ordered his command:** *MCIW*, 306; Brown, "Battle of Birch Coulie"; Boyd, "What a Boy Saw"; Sheehan, "Report of Notes"; "Sketches Historical."

63 **From the deep coulie:** *MCIW*, 308–9; Sheehan, "Report of Notes"; "Sketches Historical"; Carley, *Sioux Uprising*, 50; Egan, "Battle of Birch Coulie," 5; Anderson and Woolworth, *Through Dakota Eyes*, 152; Daniels, "Indian Outbreak," 15.

63 **Once they were certain:** "Captain Grant's Account"; Egan, "Battle of Birch Coulie," 5; Carley, *Sioux Uprising*, 51; *MCIW*, 738; Emery, *Thrilling Narrative*, 121; Daniels, "Indian Outbreak," 15.

63 **Despite the enthusiasm:** Emery, *Thrilling Narrative*, 121.

64 **And practicing the caution:** Brown, "Battle of Birch Coulie"; "Sketches Historical"; *MCIW*, 305; Anderson and Woolworth, *Through Dakota Eyes*, 152, 164; Egan, "Battle of Birch Coulie," 5; Carley, *Sioux Uprising*, 51; Sibley to Malmros, September 4, 1862.

64 **They began jeering:** Egan, "Battle of Birch Coulie," 5; *MCIW*, 738; Anderson and Woolworth, *Through Dakota Eyes*, 152.

64 **Mankato directed thirty:** Anderson and Woolworth, *Through Dakota Eyes*, 152, 164.

64 **The first volunteer:** Schultz, *Over the Earth*, 12, 102, 115–16, 118, 197–98; Hubbard and Holcombe, *Minnesota in Three Centuries*, 349; "Descriptions of the Battle of Birch Coulie"; 1860 U.S. Census, http://heritagequest.com (accessed August 21, 2008); "Col. Sheehan Dead," *Freeborn County Standard*, July 16, 1913; "Timothy J. Sheehan," form 86, Military Service Record, Old Military and Civil Service Records, National Archives and Records Administration, Washington DC; Tom Schleck, "The Forgotten Hero," undated, unpublished manuscript, Fort Ridgely State Park, Fairfax MN; Rev. Edward Neill, *History of Freeborn County* (Minneapolis: Minnesota Historical Company, 1882), 397–98; *MCIW*, 233, 245, 258–60, 731; Carley, *Sioux Uprising*, 33–35; Webb and Swedberg, *Redwood*, 46–47, 63; Sheehan, "Report of Notes"; Earle, "Reminiscences," 20–21; Goodell, "Personal Recollections," 15, 37; Anderson and Woolworth, *Through Dakota Eyes*, 137, 154; Anderson, *Little Crow*, 143–44; Heard, *History of the Sioux War*, 83.

66 **The two men, McPhail and Sheehan:** Carley, *Sioux Uprising*, 51; *MCIW*, 306; Sheehan, "Report of Notes"; "Captain Grant's Account."

67 **Alternatively, it was less:** Wedge, *History of Renville County*, 163; Gilman, *Henry Hastings Sibley*, 60, 95; Webb and Swedberg, *Redwood*, 29, 67, 93–94 (map, picture); Heard, *History of the Sioux War*, 15; Oehler, *Great Sioux Outbreak*, 66, 69; Grover Singley, *Tracing Minnesota's Old Government Roads* (St. Paul: Minnesota Historical Society, 1974), 2–3, 5; *MCIW*, 302; Daniels, "Indian Outbreak," 17; Ellig interview, September 19, 2008; Earle, "Reminiscences," 2, 14–15; *Collections of the Minnesota Historical Society*, vol. 9, 20.

67 **If Indians saw him:** Mayer, *With Pen and Pencil*, 183; "Birch Coulie Battle Called the Crux"; "Captain Grant's Account."

68 **A boyish recruit:** Brown, "Battle of Birch Coulie."

68 **He was moving at a steady gallop:** Brown, "Battle of Birch Coulie"; Sheehan, "Report of Notes."

69 **While his horse drank:** Sheehan, "Report of Notes."

69 **As soon as Sheehan accomplished:** *MCIW*, 309; Carley, *Sioux Uprising*, 51.

69 **"I have met the Indians":** *MCIW*, 309, 350; Carley, *Sioux Uprising*, 51.

7. Dr. Daniels

70 **By nightfall the men:** Buck, *Indian Outbreaks*, 236; Dakota Trial Records, "Testimony of Godfrey," http://www.law.umkc.edu.faculty/

projects/trials/Dakota/Godfrey (accessed August 13, 2008); Oehler, *Great Sioux Outbreak*, 174; Anderson and Woolworth, *Through Dakota Eyes*, 91–92, 150–51, 158.

71 **In anticipation of that attack:** Egan, "Battle of Birch Coulie," 6; Emery, *Thrilling Narrative*, 122; Lord, *They Fought for the Union*, 154–55.

71 **They periodically called:** MCIW, 738; Egan, "Battle of Birch Coulie," 6; "Birch Coulie as Taken from Memoirs"; Boyd, "Battle of Birch Coulie: A Continuance"; Oehler, *Great Sioux Outbreak*, 174; Earle, "Reminiscences," 32.

71 **Now that it was pitch dark:** Boyd, "Indian War Outbreak," 13–14; Anderson and Woolworth, *Through Dakota Eyes*, 151.

72 **Unaware that Lieutenant Sheehan:** Emery, *Thrilling Narrative*, 122; Mayer, *With Pen and Pencil*, 183; "Pony Express," http://en.wikipedia .org (accessed August 19, 2008); Mayer, *With Pen and Pencil*, 183.

72 **At sunset the horse:** "Bloodshed at Birch Coulie"; Boyd, "Indian War Outbreak," 14; Emery, *Thrilling Narrative*, 122; MCIW, 308; "Captain Grant's Account."

72 **Corporal James Auge:** Emery, *Thrilling Narrative*, 12, 117, 123; "Bloodshed at Birch Coulie"; Boyd, "Indian War Outbreak," 14; Anderson and Woolworth, *Through Dakota Eyes*, 166; Boyd, "Battle of Birch Coulie: A Wounded Man's Description," 14.

73 **Auge lifted one foot:** "Bloodshed at Birch Coulie."

73 **Suddenly, flashes of heat lightning:** Emery, *Thrilling Narrative*, 123; "Bloodshed at Birch Coulie"; Boyd, "Indian War Outbreak," 14; Anderson and Woolworth, *Through Dakota Eyes*, 1.

73 **Robert Boyd lay:** Boyd, "Indian War Outbreak," 13; Boyd, "Battle of Birch Coulie: A Continuance."

73 **Sometime after nightfall:** Boyd, "Indian War Outbreak," 13–14.

74 **The wounded men were paired:** MCIW, 738; Egan, "Battle of Birch Coulie," 6; "Birch Coulie as Taken from Memoirs"; Boyd, "Battle of Birch Coulie: A Continuance."

74 **Major Brown, drifting:** Boyd, "Battle of Birch Coulie: A Continuance"; Emery, *Thrilling Narrative*, 116; Daniels, "Indian Outbreak," 15.

74 **It was almost midnight:** "Bloodshed at Birch Coulie"; Boyd, "Battle of Birch Coulie: A Continuance"; MCIW, 317, 329; Carley, *Sioux Uprising*,

47–48; Oehler, *Great Sioux Outbreak*, 127; Hubbard and Holcombe, *Minnesota in Three Centuries*, 349; "Daniels Obituary," *Berlin Independent*, May 4, 1898; "The History of Medicine," http://www.mnwelldir.org (accessed October 7, 2008); "Dr. Jared Daniels," http://www.mnhs.org/library (accessed September 17, 2008); Flandreau, *Battle of Birch Coulie*, 427; Daniels, "Indian Outbreak," 1, 3, 6, 9, 11–12; William Gresham, ed., *Index for the History of Nicollet and Le Sueur Counties, Minnesota* (Indianapolis: Bowen, 1916), 313–14; "Dr. Jared Waldo Daniels," *St. Peter Tribune*, May 11, 1904; George Shrady, Thomas Stedman, and W. Wood, *Medical Record* (New York: Wood, 1904), 821–22; Daniels, "Indian Outbreak," 3, 9; "Pioneer Physician Dead," *St. Peter Herald*, May 6, 1904; Emery, *Thrilling Narrative*, 116; Earle, "Reminiscences," 32; "Closeup of Surgical Kit Belonging to Dr. Abel Houston Thayer," http://www.civilwarpreservations.com/newmus150B (accessed September 11, 2008); interview with Dr. Roger Christgau, Austin MN, September 24, 2008; http://www.civilwarhome.com/medicinehistory (accessed September 2008); "Civil War Battlefield Surgery," http://eHistory.osu.edu/uscw/features/medicine/cwsugeon.

77 **Then he spotted Boyd:** Boyd, "Indian War Outbreak," 8, 12–13; "Closeup of Surgical Kit"; Boyd, "Battle of Birch Coulie: A Wounded Man's Description"; Earle, "Reminiscences," 32; *MCIW*, 309; "Captain Grant's Account"; "Civil War Battlefield Surgery"; *MCIW*, 317; Jack Coggins, *Arms and Equipment of the Civil War* (New York: Fairfax Press, 1983), 117.

8. The Messenger

78 **Back at Fort Ridgely:** *MCIW*, 309, 350; Carley, *Sioux Uprising*, 51; "Veteran Writes New Version."

79 **In the attack of the day before:** "Captain Grant's Account"; *MCIW*, 309, 738.

80 **At 5:00 a.m.:** Anderson and Woolworth, *Through Dakota Eyes*, 151.

80 **From the deep grass:** Anderson and Woolworth, *Through Dakota Eyes*, 151, 164, 166; Boyd, "Indian War Outbreak," 14; *MCIW*, 309; Anderson, *Little Crow*, 155; Emery, *Thrilling Narrative*, 117.

80 **Again, Grant turned:** Anderson and Woolworth, *Through Dakota Eyes*, 164; Boyd, "Indian War Outbreak," 14; Emery, *Thrilling Narrative*, 117–18; *MCIW*, 309; Anderson, *Little Crow*, 155.

81 **The half-bloods were left:** Emery, *Thrilling Narrative*, 118, 121; Boyd, "Indian War Outbreak," 14.

82 **It was an easy decision:** MCIW, 309; Schultz, *Over the Earth*, 198; Anderson and Woolworth, *Through Dakota Eyes*, 160–61, 164; Boyd, "Indian War Outbreak," 14; Emery *Thrilling Narrative*, 118.

82 **Auge walked back:** Anderson and Woolworth, *Through Dakota Eyes*, 164; Emery, *Thrilling Narrative*, 118–21.

83 **Grant turned to the soldiers:** MCIW, 309; Anderson and Woolworth, *Through Dakota Eyes*, 166.

83 **Warriors on horseback:** MCIW, 309; Emery, *Thrilling Narrative*, 123; Boyd, "Battle of Birch Coulie: A Continuance"; Egan, "Battle of Birch Coulie," 6; Boyd, "Indian War Outbreak," 14.

83 **This time the cannon fire:** Sibley to Malmros, September 4, 1862; MCIW, 306, 309, 350, 738; Anderson and Woolworth, *Through Dakota Eyes*, 152; Goodell, "Personal Recollections," 50–51; "Veteran Writes New Version"; Carley, *Sioux Uprising*, 51; Boyd, "Indian War Outbreak," 14; Emery, *Thrilling Narrative*, 123–24; Boyd, "Battle of Birch Coulie: A Continuance"; Heard, *History of the Sioux War*, 133; Brown, "Battle of Birch Coulie"; "Captain Grant's Account"; Heard, *History of the Sioux War*, 133.

84 **Initially Dakota forces:** Heard, *History of the Sioux War*, 133; Carley, *Sioux Uprising*, 51; MCIW, 309, 350; "Veteran Writes New Version"; Anderson and Woolworth, *Through Dakota Eyes*, 153.

85 **When the colonel marched:** MCIW, 306, 350; Carley, *Sioux Uprising*, 51; Daniels, "Indian Outbreak," 15–16; Boyd, "What a Boy Saw"; "Veteran Writes New Version"; Heard, *History of the Sioux War*, 134–37; Emery, *Thrilling Narrative*, 124–25; Egan, "Battle of Birch Coulie," 6; Gilman, *Henry Hastings Sibley*, 179; Moore, "Reminiscences"; "Member of Grant's Command"; Anderson and Woolworth, *Through Dakota Eyes*, 153.

85 **Among the wounded:** Boyd, "Battle of Birch Coulie: A Wounded Man's Description"; Boyd, "Battle of Birch Coulie: A Continuance"; Boyd, "Indian War Outbreak," 15; Boyd, "What a Boy Saw."

9. Little Paul

87 **Little Crow rode east** Carley, *Sioux Uprising*, 49; Schultz, *Over the Earth*, 202, 204–7; Anderson, *Little Crow*, 154–55.

88 **Sibley left a note:** *MCIW*, 309, 350–51; Earle, "Reminiscences," 32–33; "Captain Grant's Account"; Goodell, "Personal Recollections," 50; Carley, *Sioux Uprising*, 51, 55; Emery, *Thrilling Narrative*, 124–25; Anderson and Woolworth, *Through Dakota Eyes*, 168, 173–74, 189; Anderson, *Little Crow*, 154–56; Oehler, *Great Sioux Outbreak*, 186, 188.

89 **Criers came through:** Schultz, *Over the Earth*, 208, 218; Anderson, *Little Crow*, 154–56; Anderson and Woolworth, *Through Dakota Eyes*, 168, 173.

90 **That night Little Crow:** Anderson and Woolworth, *Through Dakota Eyes*, 168, 174–76, 197; Schultz, *Over the Earth*, 212–15, 219; Anderson, *Little Crow*, 156, 158; *MCIW*, 742.

91 **The truth was:** Anderson, *Little Crow*, 157–58; Schultz, *Over the Earth*, 219; Anderson and Woolworth, *Through Dakota Eyes*, 174.

91 **Back at Fort Ridgely:** Anderson and Woolworth, *Through Dakota Eyes*, 239; author's tour of Fort Ridgely State Park, Fairfax MN, September 20, 2008; Gilman, *Henry Hastings Sibley*, 179.

92 **Sibley finally moved:** Anderson and Woolworth, *Through Dakota Eyes*, 239–41; Schultz, *Over the Earth*, 223; Carley, *Sioux Uprising*, 57; Heard, *History of the Sioux War*, 304.

93 **As soon as Sibley's expedition:** Anderson and Woolworth, *Through Dakota Eyes*, 92, 219, 222, 231, 235–36, 238, 245; Anderson, *Little Crow*, 158; Schultz, *Over the Earth*, 228–30; Alanson, "Stirring Adventures," 17; Buck, *Indian Outbreaks*, 25.

94 **Instead, the result for the Dakotas:** Carley, *Sioux Uprising*, 59; "Veteran Writes New Version"; Daniels, "Indian Outbreak," 18; Anderson, *Little Crow*, 160–61; Anderson and Woolworth, *Through Dakota Eyes*, 136–37, 219, 222, 255, 271; Alanson, "Stirring Adventures," 17; Hughes, *Indian Chiefs*, 66–67, 69; Schultz, *Over the Earth*, 236; "Sketches Historical."

94 **After the victory:** Anderson, *Little Crow*, 239–40.

95 **Still, Colonel Sibley waited:** Alanson, "Stirring Adventures," 17; Anderson, *Little Crow*, 229; Schultz, *Over the Earth*, 237; Anderson and Woolworth, *Through Dakota Eyes*, 221, 224–25, 256; Heard, *History of the Sioux War*, 181–87; Gilman, *Henry Hastings Sibley*, 183; Carley, *Sioux Uprising*, 62.

95 **Joe Coursolle spotted:** "Captain Grant's Account"; Anderson and

Woolworth, *Through Dakota Eyes*, 189–90; "List of Captives Delivered Up to Col. Sibley," *St. Paul Weekly Press*, October 19, 1862; "Col. Sibley's Dispatches," *Saint Paul Pioneer*, October 3, 1862.

95 **The government's ruse:** Anderson and Woolworth, *Through Dakota Eyes*, 226; Gilman, *Henry Hastings Sibley*, 190.

96 **A five-man military commission:** Carley, *Sioux Uprising*, 62–63; Anderson and Woolworth, *Through Dakota Eyes*, 62, 221; "Sketches Historical"; Buck, *Indian Outbreaks*, 263; "The Indian Massacres and War of 1862," *Harper's Weekly*, June 1863.

96 **As a result of the hearings:** Buck, *Indian Outbreaks*, 263; Anderson and Woolworth, *Through Dakota Eyes*, 227, 233, 264.

97 **In the fall of 1862:** Heard, *History of the Sioux War*, 344; Daniels, "Indian Outbreak," 22; Carley, *Sioux Uprising*, 64; Schultz, *Over the Earth*, 267; *MCIW*, 748; Oehler, *Great Sioux Outbreak*, 218; Buck, *Indian Outbreaks*, 264, 266; "Records of the Trials of Indians and Half-Breeds Charged with Participation in the Sioux Outbreak of 1862," MHS.

97 **For the condemned a huge square wooden scaffold:** "Execution of 38 Sioux," *Mankato Daily Review*, December 26, 1896; "The First Fifty Years of Recorded Weather"; Buck, *Indian Outbreaks*, 269; scaffold sketch, Watson Papers, Correspondence, February 1, 1863, MHS; Blegen, *Minnesota*, 469.

98 **On the evening of July 3:** "The First Fifty Years of Recorded Weather"; "Col. Sibley's Dispatches"; Webb and Swedberg, *Redwood*, 104, 111; Anderson and Woolworth, *Through Dakota Eyes*, 40, 178, 272, 280–81; Anderson, *Little Crow*, 5, 7, 176–77; Heard, *History of the Sioux War*, 307–8, 312; Carley, *Sioux Uprising*, 68; Oehler, *Great Sioux Outbreak*, 228–29; "Sketches Historical"; Charles Bryant and Abel Murch, *Indian Massacre in Minnesota: History of the Great Massacre by the Sioux Indians in Minnesota*, 2nd ed. (Chicago: Rickey and Carroll, 1864), 501–3 (scanned copy at Digital Scanning, http://www.digital-scanning.com).

10. Epilogues

100 **Eighty-five-year-old Robert K. Boyd:** "Big Program at Birch Coulie Monument," *Franklin Tribune*, August 28, 1930; Webb and Swedberg, *Redwood*, 175, 213; Sherman, *Plains Folk*, 4, 16, 25; Raban, *Bad Land*, 29, 31; Eric Bergeson, *Pirates of the Prairie* (West Des Moines: Myers House, 2008), 37.

101 **After the fight he had lain:** Boyd, "Battle of Birch Coulie: A Wounded Man's Description," 9; Boyd, "Battle of Birch Coulie: A Continuance"; Boyd, "Indian War Outbreak," 13, 17; "Sixth Regiment"; "Bertha Detloff & Robert K. Boyd," http://genforum.geneal ogy.com/detloff (accessed August 24, 2008); "Battle of Birch Coulie Was the Crux."

101 **Little Crow was dead:** Oehler, *Great Sioux Outbreak*, 231; Anderson, *Little Crow*, 178; Schultz, *Over the Earth*, 273.

101 **For Gray Bird:** Oehler, *Great Sioux Outbreak*, 224–25; Anderson and Woolworth, *Through Dakota Eyes*, 144; Webb and Swedberg, *Redwood*, 437.

102 **Chief Red Iron:** Hughes, *Indian Chiefs*, 100–101.

102 **After peace and order:** Hughes, *Indian Chiefs*, 86–87, 256; Anderson and Woolworth, *Through Dakota Eyes*, 256.

103 **Despite criticism leveled:** Anderson and Woolworth, *Through Dakota Eyes*, 67; Gilman, *Henry Hastings Sibley*, 206, 223, 231; MCIW, 712–13.

103 **After the Battle of Birch Coulie, Joseph:** "Joe Coursolle"; Anderson and Woolworth, *Through Dakota Eyes*, 57, 160, 164, 275.

104 **For almost thirty years:** Schultz, *Over the Earth*, 200; "Captain Grant's Account"; MCIW, 306–8, 310.

104 **After the captives:** Oehler, *Great Sioux Outbreak*, 219, 240; Webb and Swedberg, *Redwood*, 113, 115; Anderson and Woolworth, *Through Dakota Eyes*, 21, 234, 237; "Fort Ridgely: A Journal of the Past," Fort Ridgely State Park, Fairfax MN.

105 **Dr. Jared Daniels:** Flandreau, *Battle of Birch Coulie*, 427, 429; Earle, "Reminiscences," 32; Daniels, "Indian Outbreak," 4, 22; Charles Flandreau, *Encyclopedia of Biography of Minnesota*, vol. 1 (Chicago: Century Publishing, 1906), 427–30; "Letter from the Secretary of the Interior, Transmitting Report of Commissioners on Claims" (Washington DC: Government Printing Office, 1864), 395–97; Gresham, *Index for the History*, 313–14; Donnelly, "History of the Indian War," 212.

106 **After the Battle of Birch Coulie, Lieutenant:** Sheehan, "Report of Notes"; Neill, *History of Freeborn County*, 398; "Col. Sheehan Dead"; Timothy J. Sheehan, form 86, Military Service Record; MCIW, 275, 286; Timothy J. Sheehan Papers, MHS; Schleck, "Forgotten Hero," 8–9,

11–12; Deposition, December 21, 1907, Sheehan Memoirs, Fort Ridgely State Park, Fairfax MN; Obituary, *Minneapolis Journal*, July 15, 1913.

108 **The introduction for Boyd:** There is no surviving text of Boyd's Labor Day speech of 1930 at Birch Coulie. My reconstruction of his remarks is drawn from numerous speeches he gave on other occasions on the same subject, the texts for which are cited here: Boyd, "Battle of Birch Coulie: A Continuance"; Boyd, "Battle of Birch Coulie: A Wounded Man's Description"; "Thousands Attend B.C. Celebration," *Franklin Tribune*, September 9, 1926; "Large Gathering at Birch Coulie," *Franklin Tribune*, June 3, 1926; "Big Program at Birch Cooley Monument"; Robert K. Boyd, "Early Conditions of the Chippewa Valley," June 8, 1921, speech given at Eau Claire WI, http://Wisconsin.history .org.cgi-fin/show/file (accessed August 24, 2008); "Survivor Tells of Indian Warfare"; Buck, *Indian Outbreaks*, 283; "Battle of Birch Coulie Memorial"; Brown, "Battle of Birch Coulie"; "The Monuments: Birch Coulee Monument," RCHS; Bernard Ederer, *Birch Coulie* (New York: Exposition Press, n.d.), 10; Merrill Jarcow, *Like Father, Like Son: The Gilfillan Story* (Redwood Falls: Renville County Historical Society, n.d.), 7; Editorial, *Franklin Tribune*, April 21, 1927; "Robert Knowles Boyd," http://mnhs.org/library/find aids/00019 (accessed August 24, 2008); Robert K. Boyd to Frank Hopkins, May 30, 1930, Fort Ridgely State Park, Fairfax MN; "Battle of Birch Coulie Was the Crux"; Boyd, "What a Boy Saw"; Boyd, "Indian War Outbreak," 8.

112 **Two years later:** "Robert Knowles Boyd."

112 **In 1978 plans were laid:** "Birch Coulee Battlefield: Master Development Plan," September 1978, MHS; "Developing History: Birch Coulie Battlefield Restoration Project Is Underway," *Redwood Gazette*, May 11, 1998; "A Beautiful Place to Camp: Birch Coulie Still Bares Scars of Battle," *Redwood Gazette*, June 26, 2000.

113 **Farm neighbors:** "To Her, It's a Dirty Word," *Minneapolis Tribune*, October 4, 1995; "Students Improvise a Mud Slide at Birch Coulie," picture, *Redwood Gazette*, May 25, 2000.

113 **Further, some scientists:** Webb and Swedberg, *Redwood*, 4; "Birth of the Birch Coulee."